ARRIVAL PRESS

CRIMES AGAINST THE PLANET

Edited

By

TIM SHARP

First published in Great Britain in 1996 by
ARRIVAL PRESS
1 - 2 Wainman Road, Woodston,
Peterborough, PE2 7BU

SB ISBN 1 85786 409 3
HB ISBN1 85786 414 X

Foreword

The contents of this book concentrates on the issues of the demise and decay of our natural environment. The poets give their view in verse on the terrible issues of pollution and mis-use of our natural resources.

Whilst editing this book it became apparent how much we really do care about our unique planet Earth.

After reading this book I'm sure you will agree with the authors and share in their powerful poems and emotions, making all of us aware that we must stop this self-destruction, and fight against the *Crimes Against the Planet*.

Tim Sharp
Editor

CONTENTS

POLAR POEM

Blade-edged chunks snapped off great glaciers,
Frozen continents and oceans
Blockade the fjords with massive pack-ice,
Towering icebergs,
And threaten shipping, coastlines;

While rumbling under planet's crust
Explosive power accumulates,
Prepares to burst through mountain summits,
Rupture ice-caps, blast whole islands,
Pour down streams of molten stone
To drown, burn, totally demolish
Homesteads, hamlets, townships
In exterminating red-hot torrents.

And Hades chuckles -
A menace of volcanic cauldrons
Bubbling with infernal mud.
Geysers suddenly shoot skywards.
Geothermal thunder lies in wait
To tumble buildings, tear Earth's surface,
Crumble cliffs, hurl huge rocks about.

Yet it is God, the great creator (great destroyer),
Who plans all this;
So we ourselves are surely made
In His (sic) image.

For we too never cease to deal out death;
And we too have in store
Such genocidal bomb-blast power
That the nuclear explosions we can detonate
Could end all life
And pulverise our globe.

P Arrowsmith

THE WORLD ITSELF

The world is a wonderful fascinating place,
With different kinds of nature, symbols and race
It owns the sea, land, creatures and air,
And it's not just a planet used as a spare.

The sea brings the water to moisten the crust,
Which the air desires but can only lust
The land is for nature and to keep us alive,
Which also provides food to help us survive.

Nature treats are spoiled by race,
Who think that this beauty is seizing the space
The trees and animals are becoming afear,
Of these monstrous people who are unable to steer.

Yet we have much to learn of what the earth can
behold,
Which the sea and the land are worthy to unfold
Think what we've lost and nothing more to gain,
That destroying the earth has caused us pain.

Abbi Desborough

EARTH MAN

What are we doing to this beautiful place,
With our selfish divisions, greed and crime.
Take a good look from outer-space,
You'll know we're running out of time.

To continue like this is to lose the race,
Returning to dust and slime.
Suffer the guilt, we're all to blame,
We deserve to lose this silly game!

Paul Corrigan

2

MAN - THE FOOL

The World was black and storms arose,
Lightning flashed and blizzards blowed
How strange my friend now years have passed,
That Man should wander that way back.
He heads the way, the way he came,
From Nature's past to nature again.
If only Man could stop and see,
That only he can love like he.
We have a World of light and joy,
What fools we'd be if we destroyed,
The best form of living Man e'er knew,
It seems like folly, does it seem to you?

Paul Sanders

WE ALL MAKE MISTAKES

Once our planet was a beautiful place,
People did not live in the rat race.
The water ran as clear as crystal,
and life was lived at a leisurely pace.
Vegetation was lush and green,
the rivers, oceans and seas were clean.
Lots of fish and crustaceans,
Dolphins, whales and seals, (not mutations)
They cut down the rain forests,
but did not plant more trees.
So mud slides wiped out whole communities.
They found a hole in the ozone layer,
they say it's getting bigger.
So they tell us it's the gas we use in our sprays.
Scientists were given a free hand,
Their efforts have altered the natural balance of the land,
and now future generations will have to pay,
for all the mistakes made by man's way.

Kathrine Summers

THE EARTH COULD BE

What a wonderful planet earth
could be
If humans could only see
How they smother and torture this
marvellous place
It's a shame to belong to the human
race.

Smoke fills the beautiful skies
Gasses and fumes are a sin
The ozone layer could recover if
Humans would resolve to begin
The dangers of such deadly things.

We could wake up to clean air
Our lives would be anew, if only
Humans could change their ways,
The planet earth would be, such a
view, from an alien's point of view.

Linda Greenberg

MAN OF MANY POISONS

Don't fill the sea with oil
Fisherman fishing in watery soil,
Danger sunning harmful rays
Will man ever learn better ways?
Earth's on loan till man's extinct,
Pull together, united linked
Stop this silly mad destruction
Man-made weapons of seduction.

Joe Kay

A CHILD WONDERS

I wonder why the earth is round
When to me it looks quite flat.
I wonder why the sky is blue
There must be a reason for that.

I wonder why the grass is green
And why trees grow so tall
I suppose it would not be quite right
If the same things applied to all.

I wonder why dinosaurs became extinct
After millions of years of existence,
Why microbes seem to go on forever
There seems no end to their persistence.

I wonder when the world will end
In God's good time, or ours?
There's so much atomic energy round
And in the hands of so many Powers.

I wonder why we have to die
Why our time on earth's so short
To take our place in Heaven or Hell?
At least, that's what I've been taught.

I wonder why there's so much hate
Cruelty, pain and greed
And in a world of plenty
Man's caused so very much need.

I really wonder what God must think
Of how man's treated His planet
He intended it to be His pride and joy
Since the day when He began it.

William M Jones

OUR COUNTRY

We were a very proud country,
We could hold our heads up high.
Our fore fathers and mothers, they fought for us and died,
They died and suffered to put this country where it is today.
We fought every country that went against us,
And we were victorious all of the way.

As the time went by our country got back on its feet.
Our wealth, our businesses, flourish,
Our economy became very thrifty,
Our prosperity grew, and grew.
There was business, and jobs for everybody,
And oh boy it was the best in the world.

Now as the years flew by,
Our country should have even got better,
But instead it went down the drain.
The government just pulled the plug out,
And of course they just washed it all the way.

They sold our country out,
Our wealth, and our dignity, and our pride.
They sold us to some of the countries,
Who we fought against in the past,
Okay, but let us own our own country,
But first they put us into the Common Market,
And they change our pound, shilling, pence,
Turned it into decimal coinage, and oh boy, didn't it do well?

They brought out the cutbacks,
Then everything ran down,
And even lots of things fell down.
They have practically changed all of our way of life.
You name it they changed it.

So please for all of us,
Let us go back to like it was in the past.
Like our namesake,

Great Britain. The best in the world.

Margaret Coleman

THROUGH THE WORLD'S EYES

The great big world keeps on turning
It has seen many changes through the years
Turning alone it reviews the situation
With the corruption, wars, slaughter and tears.

Having no power to control right or wrong
Just watching closely until the end of time
Each new generation living their lives from day to day
Like a monument the world stays proud and sublime

Seeing the ruins where once stood grand castles
People suffering through famine and parched deserts of sand
Wars with the bloodshed have contributed to this destruction
Countries are being crushed beyond repair, by man's hand.

The great big world's sad eyes, see all this turmoil and pain
It hopes one day peace will prevail on earth once more
As it turns in the universe wondering how much time is left
Surviving yet another day seeing suffering, just like the day before.

To live in peace all nations must change their ways
Unless evil is stopped now, the great big world can never alter
Soon, with total disaster, the world will crumble and die
Destroyed by man's hand, not by fire or water.

Brenda Colvin

DESTRUCTION

Once there were fields of rolling hills
hedges layed with olden skills
spotted orchids here and there
perfume of bluebells in the air
Once there were farms and cottages small
Now no longer there at all
all were added to . . . to change
into a modern country grange.
For the owners then to send
friends down just for the weekend
Folks who come in from the town
and turn the country upside down
Round the corners driving fast
not caring how we all get past
Once you need not lock the door
this you can't do any more.
Can this be the march of time
ending with a world of crime?
Afraid to go out after dark,
afraid to venture to the park.
Now the world is full of greed
selfishness and endless speed.
What would our forefathers say
if they could come back today?

Ann Boyd

MANKIND ON TRIAL

The trees now burnt
The bracken bare
Where once nature's beauty had been seen
Now an empty barren wasteland
Lies deserted of life
Upon our planet earth.
Its atmosphere now poisoned
By polluted skies
Unclean
Forests decaying
Rivers run dry
Contaminated oceans now destroyed
By the hand of man
Society's shame
Questions must be asked
Who is to blame
Before the end result
Is the destruction of earth itself.

Arthur Harvey

ECOLOGY

I laughed and laughed until I cried
And put my prune stones on the side
My plate was huge - 'twas like a planet
They thought of me a hungry gannet
'I'll eat this meal then if I must'
And sank my teeth in the earth's crust

Julia Wallis-Bradford

9

TEARS FOR A CROW

The mother crow she flew
So high,
With straw in beak she
Circled by,
Confusion grew as home
She neared,
The tree had gone with the chicks
She'd reared,
Her load was dropped with stress
She cried,
Yes, she knew her young
Had died,
In vain she searched above
The crowd,
For the home of which she was
So proud,
Man had felled and stolen
Her world,
As to the ground life's reason
Was hurled.
One day soon she'll begin
To rebuild,
Her purpose in life can never
Be killed.

On that day my tears
Did flow,
My heart it ached for the
Mother crow,
The green thing just got in
The way,
Against beauteous nature man had
His say.

Pauline Jones

PLIGHT OF THE EARTH

When will man understand
The plight of the earth?
She cries out to help her
For all her worth
Why won't we listen
And lend her a hand?
We don't need the pollution
That covers our land
Look what she's given
Over the years
All we are giving her
Seems to be tears
Rain forests disappear
Under our nose
What if a child should ask
'What is a rose?'
The way it's going, this day will come
And all man will say is
What's done is done
No more elephants roaming free
All the whales have gone from the sea
We have the power to put things right
Need to keep trying not give up the fight.

Janis Smith

IT COULD HAVE BEEN EDEN . . .

There once was a time when forests grew, lush and green and rife.
Breathing unpolluted air we believed was a way of life.
Eating the meal upon our plate without the fear of harm
instead of contamination, instead of the ruined farm.
We could have had an Eden, we could have had it all
we are simply the caretakers, not the Lord of the Hall.
Nature has given us all we need, all is there if we seek.
But we think that we're the masters. We're children, and we're weak.
We label our problems 'environment', ask where the problems start.
It was us, *we* raped the planet, and tore out her loving heart.
And when we yell pollution, carcinogens and the like,
we put them there, not nature. *We* made the deadly strike.
We slashed and burned the forests, we contaminate the soil
we gouged our her coal and peat and wood, made her spew out
$\qquad\qquad\qquad\qquad\qquad$ the precious oil.
Look at the sun! We don't see warmth or friendliness or hope
but melanomas, cancers, oh, there's such a lot of scope.
We're playing with radiation - nothing to see or feel
nothing to hear or touch my friend. At least, not until you're ill.
Then you can see what man has done, in his apocalyptic way
he's messed into what he shouldn't, like delinquent brats at play.
We've shown just how much she can trust us, we've opened a hole in the sky.
How much bigger does it need to be until we all start to fry?
She gave us everything we need, the forests, the pastures, the sea
the rivers and streams the mountains and dales, an Eden for you and me.
All *we* had to do was love her, this wonderful planet called earth.
More effort, more planning, less stripping her bare, let's try
$\qquad\qquad\qquad\qquad\qquad$ for all that we're worth.
Or all that we'll leave to the future, all that remains of this glory
will fade into desolation, where they'll tell of the trees as a story.
Along with the grass and the flowers, together with brooks and the seas,
legend is all that we vandals will leave, instead we should drop to our knees.
And pray there is still a flicker of hope, and that we can right the sin
of erasing the things that make living worthwhile, and try to learn
$\qquad\qquad\qquad\qquad\qquad$ how to begin.

Rosemarie Varndell

12

WHAT HAVE WE DONE?

There are so many crimes committed by man that I don't know
where to start,
With all our combined actions we have torn this planet apart.
Killing many animals that get in our way,
So that many species are extinct today.

Buildings are being put up everywhere,
They are being built on fields that used to be there.
Forests are being cut down hundreds at a time,
And that is only a few of man's crimes.

We have thrown out nature's balance,
And we are not giving the planet a chance.
All we have done is take,
And we are now paying for our mistake.

We have never given anything back,
And we can't go on like that.
We have filled the planet with our pollution,
And like this we can't carry on.

We are killing the planet,
And it is something we are starting to regret.
We must change our ways fast,
If we want this planet to last.

The planet is getting revenge for what we have done,
We are now paying for all the centuries of destruction.
And if we want to save our own lives,
We must help this planet to survive.

We have stripped the planet of its natural resources,
We have created a great mess.
This dying planet we must mend,
If we are to save ourselves in the end.

Katharine Hall

STICKS AND STONES

Sticks and bricks and walls and stones
Every upward rising
Nature flattened underfoot
Suppressed in concrete binding

Traffic, honking, roaring, pouring
Thundering blundering by
The dust-filled eye of sun looks from
A subdued, brick-framed sky

People hurrying hither, thither
Ants upon a street
A mad cacophony of sound
A million restless feet

Will one day nature rise in might
And wrench us from her back;
Hurl us into extinction
And have the last grim laugh?

Sybil Sibthorpe

THE TEARS OF A CHILD

A fragile new life, breathes upon the snow.
And sad dark eyes glisten, with temperatures so low.
New life is a wonder, shared with a mother's love.
Across this frozen desert, it thrives with God above.

Then a strange shape beckons from the sea.
It's man who brought the knowledge, and where he wants to be.
'Come fight me' shouts the warrior, at his feet where he lies.
But the pup looks up helplessly, and tears he cries.

14

We are shaken by the silence when the men are gone
All their work for profit, riches that they long.
A shadow cast of darkness, by the sun as it appears.
All that's left is puddles, of saddened brimming tears.

Just tears across the snow, nothing else remains,
Soiled with the hands of man, his mark, his stain
The tears start to darken, then finally to red.
And slowly disappearing, as the child lies dead.

A M Lawrence

DESTINY

The rape that flowers in early April - have the seasons turned around?
Early warmth from springtime sun pushed up the buds from underground.
Some fields are green, like summertime - yet this is early spring!
The dandelions in gay profusion, snow-white daisies opening.

The bees and flies the wasps and ants, with butterflies there too;
So early in the year for insects; 'neath the warmth of skies so blue.
Do we blame this global warming for these sights which seem so rare?
What can be the explanation? Are the scientists aware?

'Greenhouse effect' is common knowledge, so often words are used -
We read them daily in the papers - on TV - are they abused?
Do we understand the meaning? Is there depth in what they say?
Is there logic in our questions? Are the answers here today?

Future years will prove the theory - or disprove - as the case may be,
Have we destroyed the ozone layer - and changed the shape of destiny?
No-one really knows the answer, time will tell what will befall,
Come down to earth - and change your ways - there'll be no planet left at all.

Jan Portlock-Barker

GLOBAL WARNING!

Four thousand million years old am I,
Please listen to my voice,
Silent I can no longer remain,
Mankind has given me no other choice.

Chemicals pollute my rivers and seas,
And finally poison the fish,
That you catch and eat for yourself,
Is this your dying wish?

Pesticides sprayed onto crops,
To help vegetation to grow,
Also damage the soil and kill the birds,
Please don't say you did not know.

Arable lands will soon be barren,
If you continue to abuse,
Through soil erosion and degradation,
Soon will be of no use.

Aeroplanes and rocket launches,
Burn fuel into the atmosphere,
Ultraviolet rays can now burn through,
Because you have weakened the ozone layer.

Tropical forests are disappearing,
With the flora and fauna they sustain,
Many will become extinct,
Never to be seen again.

I wait in hope it's not too late,
For the damage to be repaired,
Let rivers run clean, trees take root,
And surround ourselves with clean air.

James Gallagher

WE CARE NOT FOR OUR CRIME

We kill our trees, pollute our rivers
When will the torture end?
We are hostile to mother nature
While she regards us as a friend.

I find a place within my heart
Which is full of so much shame
I admit what others will not admit
That it is our actions to blame.

I found a friend in nature once
But now she's turned her back
And once a world so beautiful
Now our future's turned to black.

In every leaf of every tree
Its suffering tells a tale of woe
And nature's crying out to us -
Pleading to stop the fatal blow.

In every river, its tears that flow
Towards an endless sea,
Sad I am to see them flow
Crying because of you - and me.

We have upset the balance of natural life
We care not for our crime
Mother nature will not let us go unpunished
We will all surely learn in time.

Jenny Amery

OUR WORLD

Just as long as our world keeps turning
And as long as the wind blows free
As long as the valleys are lush and green
And the rivers flow down to the sea.

As long as the sun keeps shining
As long as the birds can sing
As long as the flowers can raise their heads
With the coming of the spring.

Just as long as the seasons can come and go
Each with their own intent
And a warming sun with its gentle rays
Keeps our mother earth content.

But what is the ozone gets thinner
And the blazing sun scorches the land
And our world is one vast empty desert
With no life to be seen, only sand.

And what if our world is polluted
If acid rain falls from the skies
And the fields and the valleys lay barren
As slowly our mother earth dies.

Surely we owe to our children
A future and not to deprive
So by keeping it free from pollution
We'll be helping our world to survive.

Evelyn Tilley

IF THERE'S A GOD . . .

The thin little body racked with pain.
How can God let it happen - has the world gone insane?
Famine and drought in this world of ours
Where's the miracles now and the men with power?
Arms outstretched, eyes as big as saucers.
What has she done to suffer such torture?
Helping hands reach out to embrace.
Oh God what is happening to the human race?
Tenderness, compassion, love and care
But there's not enough to go round, not enough to share.
Why is there such suffering, hunger and loss?
Ask the politicians they put it down to cost.
Why does it cost money to help people in need?
So God cut the crap . . .

Listen to the prayers . . .

take heed.

Gena McCrystal

MOTHER EARTH

A time will come when Mother Earth disowns her inhabitants, and banishes the lodgers who have disrespected and abused her for too long. Then what shall become of us?

Compared to a bright summer's day, we display nothing.

Without Mother Earth's constant replenishing of resources, we would have nothing.

In comparison to the power of Mother Earth, we are nothing.

Yet, until the day of judgement arrives, we will continue to ignore her and by then it will be too late.

C E Cruddas

POLLUTION - SOLUTION

The ozone layer is lifting
And rays are getting through
Which can harm our lovely planet
And the likes of me and you.

We're sending gas emissions
And acrid fumes into the air,
As for polluting all the rivers
Just no-one seems to care.

The Arctic ice is melting
The sea begins to rise,
Smog and chemic overspills
Spoil our lovely skies.

Our shores are lined with litter
Even worse - a sewage bin -
And ships - their oil they empty
It really is a sin.

We chop down all the rainforests
And destroy the habitat
Of rare species in the jungle
From gorilla to wild cat.

We must love our beauteous planet
And save it from these ills
Let's promote our gifted scientists
To use their clever skills.

They must have ways to save us
To recycle filth and waste
It needs to start today now
There really must be haste.

So come now make an effort
To stop pollution of our lands
We can all begin in our backyard
The solution's in our hands!

Mollie D Earl

TAKE ACTION

Our fragile earth is under stress,
Is there a solution to all this mess?
We can only hope and guess,
And treat it with our love and respect.

Global warming is a threat,
Drought brings hunger, disease and death,
Rain forests will soon be just a memory,
But too late to say we're sorry.

No-one is immune from acid rain,
It falls like poison on our plains,
What a crying shame
The sea is like a sewer and our fish a whole lot fewer.

Our children have the right to work and dream,
What hope now for their future schemes
We must all do our bit to help the environment,
To heal this turmoil, pain and torment.

We must all take our share of blame
And hang our heads in shame,
So for each and every one of us our aim must be to

take action.

G L Glanville

DESIGNER RAIN

Acid rain
Upon the trees
Water their feed
For their needs
That's for sure
Rain killing more

All trees you blight
Your watery death
Trees of might
So what is left
The woodman's axe
And it 'bites'

Your designer rain
From living man
Woodman woodman
Cut me down
My life all spent
This rain of death

Trees no more
Are we to breathe
The end you and me.

Edward T Ward

NOISE

Fans are whirring, fridges purring, is there any solution?
Aircraft droning, machines groaning, it's all noise pollution.
Sirens wailing, brakes are failing, music with a beat,
Cars and lorries, typewriters - sorry, the noise increases with the heat.

The distant rumble of the motorway, the persistent buzz of a bluebottle fly,
The clatter of lawnmowers, the chatter of children, getting louder as
time passes by.
When was the last time I listened to birdsong, or the heady droning of bees?
Or just sat in silence and read a book without the accompaniment of these?

Maria E Cornell

INHUMANITY

In the darkness of his Third World mine
Man rages as he scratches for time.
Marks the boundaries in blood so red
His bloated inhumanity fed.
He sits upon the laded table
Kicks away the chairs
Feasting on the starving's cries
And the gaunt and hungry stares.
He laughs this parasitic leech
Then casts the runes in children's bones.
His inhumanity finely honed.
Making love to his own craven image
Turned on by the blood and carnage.
Justifying his inhuman whims
By the colour of another's skin.
He throws his vipers into the pit
Curses bitterly when he gets bit
Destroying himself with festering wrath
Creating his own behemoth.
Man leaves us all eternally damned
By his inhumanity towards his fellow man.

Alene Kimm

MAN'S GREED

When people walk beneath a tree
I wonder what they really see
Don't they know that nature in her enormous plan
Didn't only plant them for the benefit of man
Must they clear the forest and let the soil erode away
Surely in this day and age there must be another way
There's pollution in the rivers where all the fishes die
There are gases in the ozone layer and a hole high in the sky
There's oil slicks in the oceans where tankers have gone down
Coating the birds with oil causing them to drown
Man's greed is spoiling all the land
Which was created by a mighty hand
What will be left for the next generation?
        Only dust and devastation.

Mary Powell

WHAT IF LITTLE FISHES NO LONGER FRY?

Trailing those long nets for many a mile
Can erase our light self-sufficient smile;
Too complacent about the price of fish
Grimacing today on the dainty dish
Of those who prefer delicate seafood
With the world in such a gluttonous mood
Depleting the oceans' God-given wealth
As poor people fear for physical health!
Now all the cod liver oil disappears
And ships' captains weep or raise hearty cheers
At vandalism against meekest mankind
Yet it is the blind who have led the blind!
Those still unborn, how will they ever cope
If we fail to bequeath them one dram of hope?

Patricia Howe

VANISHING

Lost.
Alone.
Nowhere to turn.
Life is desolation,
My mind is
Confusion.
I feel my world
Slipping away from us.
We haven't got a chance.
Beauty destroyed
Before my eyes
And, I feel our
History -
Our future -
Vanishing.

Jennifer Emery

CASE FOR THE DEFENCE

Look at me,
I am beauty.
Love me,
I am here for you.
Let your heart see my magic.
I am colour and I am darkness,
The circle of life
And death.
Resist my destruction,
I am all that you have experienced,
I am Planet Earth.

Joyce Mason

HOME SWEET HOME

'It's progress' we state,
man's evolution.
Tearing down the seeds of growth,
filling the seas with pollution.

Leaving barren wastes,
like empty minds.
No love in our hearts,
our eyes are blind.

We devour the earth,
disfigure its beauty.
Our greed is to feed,
our riches, our duty.

Open your hearts,
look around and see.
The destruction of unnatural disaster,
thanks to you and me.

Tania Varndell

OUR PLANET

Come with me down to the sea,
Where we can get covered with glee,
Swim in the effluent, dip in the tar,
Never mind the solvents, they'll just leave a scar,
Playing in the brine if the weather is fine,
Behind a mist of pollution the sun will never shine,
Then with a walk on the beach not minding our itchy feet,
Or those giant gnats, we'll be dabbing our bodies for weeks,
Snaking off down the motorway in all the car exhausts,
Did you have a lovely holiday? Of course,
And we'll crawl into bed, as the moon turns red,
For on this our planet, there's a lot to be said.

Joan McAvoy

26

USED AND ABUSED

Acid spray - fields of grey
Polluted life - brings about strife
Charred remains - aches and pains
Used world - world abused.

Fiona Stimpson

FOOLED BY THE MOON

They were all so proud to send a man,
Upon our beautiful moon
But the heavens knew like they always do,
The idea would be fraught with *doom.*

Monsoons and floods and mile high tides,
Earthquakes, and landslides abound.
Snow-capped mountains all disturbed.
Avalanches pouring down,
Lives are lost and forests destroyed,
Lava from erupted Etna,
And all earth's seasons quite confused,
While flowers lost their summer nectar.

Grandma once said, I'm telling you now,
Don't play around with the heavens,
For if you do, it'll be the worse for you,
And God will teach you a lesson.

I remember those words from an early age,
And long have they stayed with me,
For 'tis true my friend, that all that has passed,
Has come to prove her sincerity.

Audrey Simms

27

CRIMES AGAINST THE PLANET

They came in search of our free
Black rock found underground, to be
Rich from the hard work of the folk
Who laboured on beneath their yoke.

My valley then was clothed in green,
The trees, and grass could all be seen,
But mining caused great ugly scars,
The countryside pitted like Mars.

The people lived in poverty,
Life was so hard, nothing was free
Except the love and care they shared
In times of need when they were scared

Of pitfalls which might mean one day
A loved one killed, no wage to pay
For food and clothing, housing needs,
They would be treated just like weeds

Uprooted and then cast aside.
Nowhere to go. Where could they hide?
What would they eat? How would they live?
Mine owners had no time to give

A thought to them, or time to care
Just spent their time destroying fair
Green acres of the countryside.
Coal meant money and also pride.

Graveyards and slag heaps appeared,
Green pastures changed, some disappeared.
The people lived from day to day,
They knew there was no other way.

Catherine Craft

NOT A BANG, OR A WHIMPER ...

Not a bang, or a whimper
The silent earth slips away
Moored no longer to the sun
Freed by man's greed
And bad intentions
Into a universe waiting, all undone.
As the world wavers in its orbit
The oceans sway in anger
At the move
Life betrayed, deserts under water
Cheated of a future
Drained of love.
Never, in a million years
Has nature bullied
The land like this.
Charged and sentenced, doomed to die
Man, the Intelligent
Turns his back on a mother's kiss.

A L Griffin

DISASTER

Gale force winds wreaked havoc that day.
Beached a tanker in the bay.
The crew had fled and left it bare.
Rescue folk could only stare.
Its fate was sealed and worse yet
For oil it carried and did emit
Over bird and seal and beach.
A mighty lesson to us teach:
Safer methods must be found,
No more ships to run aground.
The cost to nature is too great,
So let's change now before it's too late.

George Bailey

PLANET EARTH

Look at planet Earth,
She is a precious jewel in space,
A spherical world
Beaming with love and grace.

Take a good look at planet Earth,
Because she is dying.
No more will we run
Through open forests,
And watch the sun dancing
Through the trees.
We must listen now
To the sounds of her crying.

Why do we allow man
To steal the countryside
From beneath our feet?
Fields that come alive
With wild flowers and spring lambs,
Soon will become concrete jungles.
Destruction and pollution is
Something everyone should
Want to beat.

Every step man takes
Is full of hate,
We live every day of our lives
Under the threat of
Nuclear destruction.
We must change this world
Before it's too late.

Angela Mitchell

CHEMICAL CAPERS

Compare the produce labelled thus 'organic'
With food that's grown with chemicals and care,
And you'll see without a doubt
What the fuss is all about,
For chemicals produce more wholesome fare.
The grain of wheat that's sown without protection
And grows in competition with a weed,
Will surely come to grief,
With some mildew on its leaf,
And produce a very sickly crop indeed.
The lettuce lying limp and so pathetic
Was grown without a scientific plan.
It lost its fight with thugs, bacteria and bugs,
With no protective help from modern man.
The potato in its rough and wrinkled jacket
Was fed on smelly muck and rotting waste,
And the maggot there inside
Just crawled in and promptly died,
Which doesn't help to make a pleasant taste.
For some of nature's ways are not hygienic,
The manners of a beetle can be crude,
The fruit fly drops its bits
And the aphid chews and spits
As they do their little dance upon your food.
So discard the produce labelled thus 'organic'.
Let the scientist and chemist have their way,
And the farmer should rejoice
When the bishop's booming voice
Announces from the pulpit, 'Let us spray.'

A E G Wells

FROM HERE TO IMMORTALITY

In the year 2,000 and the following centuries beyond,
Mankind's science may resemble a magician's wand,
New discoveries and inventions, will progress fast and thick,
That fantastic science of man's future, will be like magic.

Our moon's scientific bases and communities, will prosper and thrive,
Colonisation of Mars and other planets, from dreams will come alive,
Dyson Spheres' artificial created worlds, will orbit our own sun,
Controls of heredity, suspended animation, and artificial life has begun.

Robots, cyborgs, artificial intelligence, logical languages in place,
Weather control, wireless energy, transmutation, planetary mining in space,
Gravity waves detected and gravity control, global libraries, stellar flight,
Space drive vehicles achieving near light speeds, become a common sight.

Mechanical educators, memory playbacks, machine intelligence
surpasses man's,
Telesensory devices, planetary engineering, matter transmitters,
to beam down,
Earth and inter-stellar probes, leading to climate control and a world brain,
Replicators, nuclear catalysts, bio-engineering, no earth poverties remain.

Terra-forming other planets, intelligent animals, time-perception
enhancement,
Contacting and meeting with extra-terrestrials, alien cultures,
ambassadors sent,
Astronomical engineering, space-time distortion, time travel and immortality,
Waiting to be discovered by future humans, carrying genes
from you and me.

Duncan Forbes

32

OUR MOTHER EARTH

Oh Mother Earth so beautiful,
> You give us life so rare;
With nature in its many forms,
> On land and sea and air;
But man's great greed has made you sad
> By cutting down your trees;
And taking all your mineral wealth,
> And pillaging your seas.
The water that was once so clear,
> Is now unfit to drink;
And man's great greed and jealousy
> Has brought him to the brink,
Of devastating conflict,
> That threatens all of life;
And if we do not heed the signs,
> That are so clear to see,
Mother Earth will fight back soon
> To free herself of strife,
With earthquakes and with tidal waves,
> And thunderstorms severe,
To try and save this world of Hers,
> And all that She holds dear;
So man can start again some day
> Much wiser than before,
To enjoy the wealth of Mother Earth
> And respect Her much much more.

Francis A Watson

ONLY YESTERDAY

Our planet suffers from progress.
Better to dump the old car
Save on untreated sewage
Destroy another rain forest
Use the strongest insecticides
Join the instant result age.

The dark Satanic mills
Of grimy industrial towns
Now breathe a different air.
Marine birds drop with oil
Even the coral reef
Waits for someone to care.

Poor, short-sighted Mr Robinson
When the sea turned luminous
The islanders made haste.
Their sacrifice was ours
We created the clouds
And tons of toxic waste.

Aquatic life rots on the shore
The oceans are down to three,
Like long-lost wishes
Which run far too deep
We sailed that shining green.
Two hundred million years
Then suddenly - *unclean.*

Maureen Macnaughtan

POLLUTION
(For KS CW JS)

Cans, wrappers, paper bags
Black bin liners, a box of fags

A can of beer, a bottle of tonic
A school letter, a picture of Sonic

Old broken cassette player pieces
A slippery banana peel, some half-eaten cheeses

Broken fences, torn apart hedges,
Door knobs, screws, door wedges

An old school book, a 20p ring
In one corner a bird's head in the other its wing.

A piece of loose washing, an odd slipper,
Some chips with ketchup, a smelly kipper

An eyeliner pencil, a piece of wallpaper,
A magazine, a comic of a supernatural caper

A hair clip, a rusty pin
An Asda bag, a wastepaper bin.

S Rashid (14)

POLLUTED PLANET

There's not so many early morning
Songbirds, and nobody knows why.
But the thing we should take notice of
Is, the common little fly.
For when their irritating flight
Has stopped and is no more
The people on our lovely earth
Will all have reached death's door.

John Howell Roberts

PROTEST SONG

Despite our busy days
As we go our hectic ways
And rush from here to there
Madly flying,
Could we stop to contemplate
On the very parlous state
Of this countryside of ours
Sadly dying.

Pesticides have killed the bees,
Dutch elm disease the trees,
Before long it may be us
Crisply frying.
May we have the guts to shout
If we disagree about
A policy, not take it
Meekly lying.

Don't take it lying down
From MPs up in town
'Cos we've just got to keep
Ever trying.
We must get pollution banned
From this green and pleasant land.
Let our voices now be heard
Loudly crying.

Mary Ingleton

THE CITY SUMMER

From the hill, through gaps in the roadside trees
On days when the noontide sun shines bright
Brief views of misty spires come into sight.
Through a heat engendered haze unstirred by breeze,
On a stretching saffron sea, they float at ease.
Studious domes and towers of noble height,
Transformed to phantoms by the baking light,
To shimmer and dance and bow as they please
As they soar above the veils of shaded brown
That those below breathe in, as breathe they must,
The exhausted air that forms this rusty crown.
This torpid shroud of minatory dust
The dregs of ancient forests rotted down
But exhumed again, to fuel the driving lust
For powered transportation through the town.

Tom Robertson

LIFE ON MARS?

Outside this glasshouse
all we see is red.
Some ventured outside
once, now they are dead.

Contained here like rare
protected species,
shipped to Mars when Earth
was blown to pieces.

We killed our planet
and were forced to run,
Only now we see,
just what we have done.

Karen Greatbatch

MANKIND

I revisited Gibraltar and Singapore too
Finding to my horror that they were grown
Their lands weren't big enough
So claimed sand from the seabed
Wondered why the tides were higher
Or coastal cliffs were dropping back to sea

Above the cities and towns are clouds
Clouds dangerous to breathe
The beaches are polluted by what the tides spew
And vessels ignore all the laws
We wonder why temperatures are changing
Not bothering about our back gardens

Governments say one thing but do another
Backing countries fighting each other
Wars grow bigger, more innocent involved
All so that they look good - but
Medicine creates miracles
While man kills infant foetuses
Who is to blame for mankind's crime?
Each one of us, in our own stupid way.

Tilla Smith

THIS POOR WORLD

Poor tortured earth when will man see
Just how it hungers to be free
The ozone layer has lost its top
Will this madness ever stop

Man's killing earth with his modern science
When on its very being is our reliance
The earth speaks out don't you hear her cry
'If you persist in this I will surely die'

Chemicals warfare and nuclear waste
To save our world we must make haste
Against these odds our world must strive
And challenge man to stay alive

Each new invention we test with ease
Stifling the earth its life we squeeze
Man's new-found intelligence will be his fall
He'll end the world and kill us all

Eleise Waller

EARTH FOR SALE, NEEDS ATTENTION

A consumer world, consuming the earth
One more factory born, as a mother gives birth,
Killing of fields, as landfill sites grow,
Child's, once healthy face, but now, the food has a glow.
Government steals earth, one more no entry zone,
To do tests on the hole in the precious ozone.

Decimation of forests, to the very last leaf,
For nations fast food passion for burgers of beef,
The way of the west, is the way the rest want to live,
Many more millions, will take, but what will they give,
People living their dreams, all is peaches and cream.
A planet like Hollywood, life is a scream,
Till the dawn, of a nightmare, but will we awake,
Or will nature unbalanced, finally fall and then break.

The fate of the earth lies within our own power,
Do we rise to the challenge, or do we just sit and cower,
And wait for the new age, a second chance, a rebirth,
If we do, we'll be waiting till the end of the earth.

Jeffrey Crossley

IT DOESN'T MATTER

It doesn't matter
if we pump raw sewage
into the blue ocean
it's big enough -
isn't it?

It doesn't matter
if the fish float
rotting grey on the sluggish sea
there are millions of them
and we can't eat them all anyway.

It doesn't matter
if
a few species die -
what's one more animal
more or less?

It doesn't matter if our planet
dies.
There are plenty more planets
out there -
aren't there?

Benjamin Jones

RABBIT PIE

It was one of those still skies,
as if caught in a landscape
painter's eye -
The landscape itself was hardly moving
but for a young rabbit
who thought life was sweet,
hopping forward
and nibbling the fresh grass.

'There is,' said the man with a gun,
'altogether too much rabbit nibbling.'
Bang! Went the gun
and all the scuts ran -
except the young rabbit.
She/he dies,
but the sky remains.
Oh murderous sky!

Stuart Mortished

EARTHLY TORTURE

Rain of acid pours from the sky
Whilst oil spills and gushes into ready polluted oceans,
Seabirds lie dying unable to fly,
All of this makes me cry out; why?

The main reason is human greed,
We abuse and torture our once beautiful earth
In order to fulfil some capitalist economic need.
From the earth's weak and often slashed veins,
How much more can we possibly bleed?

We exploit and we take,
We maim and we rape,
All of this for money and its sake,
We chop down forests and replant with conifers,
But nature knows, this is fake.

To survive we must stop
And treat our world as our God,
We must respect this wonderful creation,
And prevent the happening
Of such wanton desecration.

Rebecca Mourton

SAVE OUR WORLD

Leafy tree that took so long,
to grow so tall and now you're gone.
Took years and years to grow so tall,
a few cruel cuts to make you fall.
How selfish we have all become
and not considered the outcome,
the rape and pillage of our lands.
The earth's destruction in our hands.
Don't treat the forests like a crop,
it's not too late but we must stop.
In all the countries and the nations,
let's save our world through conservation.

Sue Wilkinson

HUMANS VERSUS PLANET EARTH

If we so-called human beings
Keep over-crowding planet earth,
Pushing out the other creatures,
Over-estimating our own worth,
Polluting every sea and river
With our chemicals and trash,
Poisoning earth's atmosphere,
Then, one day, will come the crash.
Having killed off all the other life
In the sea, the air, on land,
What then will we be left with?
Just barren waste and sand.

Of course, we who let this happen
Will all be long since dead,
But cannot we now change our ways?
And leave earth beautiful instead.

Elsie M Whipp

42

DO SOMETHING

They say that if thine eye offends thee
Then pluck it out,
But wouldn't that leave them, so many then, rolling about
In the open spaces where once were carved lanes,
Where dwelled forest creatures
And fresh fell the rain.

With a sightless way of life there would be no point to
Manufacturing, as nobody will be able to appreciate the
End result of all that endeavour and creativity.

And since a high degree of accuracy is unnecessary for a
Sightless way of life, that just leaves recreation.
I suppose we could all play games for our amusement.
How about badminton, Mr Ridiculous?
We could glue feathers onto those useless eyeballs
And thus make cocks,
Using fish-glue derived from the sea's dwindling stocks,
And by leaving all birds flightless, and the skies empty,
They'd be easier to catch and devour,
Nature always provides for the blind of her flowers.

Perhaps in time the woods will close in,
Hemming us tighter, squeezing and pressing in their
Flourishing green - the revenge of the trees,
Their roots breaking up the contrived and distorted
Environment around us.
Eventually leaving us unable to wander about
Freely, for fear of bumping into unseen obstacles
So that in time we become too frightened
To act, or move, or do anything.

Darren Griffin

FROM PARADISE TO GENOCIDE

Look through these bullet punctured rainbows
And see a valley filled with the rusting machinery of war
Their camouflage makes their metal look like rotting flesh
There's a place where the birds refuse to sing
And the soul of murder refuse to rest.

Depleted uranium fires burn
Where the most beautiful flowers have the scent of corpses
The hot and poisoned squirming soil
Where butchered human remains protrude
See the houses burn down without screaming
These seem to be the only things which don't scream
All about me screaming children
All about me ensanguined man-made refuse.

Mother earth being raped of all resources
Food chain collapse so you eat your faeces
The polar ice caps have nearly gone
Global warming and atomic bombs
Pour uranium into the sea
Fish have cancer like you and me
Soon you will need a mask to breathe the air
And a silver suit to walk your synthetic pets.

A dark and smoking planet remains
Cut wide open for the vultures to dine
Stick their heads in and pull out mankind
Gone from paradise to genocide.

Tim Heath

CRY OF THE DOLPHINS

We dolphins let out our mournful cry,
'Please don't let our planet die.'
We have lived so long as you may know,
We have watched man come and watched him grow.
Your discoveries have been great and promised great joy,
Now they threaten to destroy.

Your youngest child discards cans and breaks jars,
Whilst your older kind pumps poisons from cars.
The female of your species is not alone,
She uses her sprays and kills the ozone.
We *try* to tell you and you pretend to hear,
You say we are clever but still we fear,
That this beautiful world once made so pure,
Cannot much longer seem to endure,
Its animals killed off in the name of science,
Missiles and bombs built in sheer defiance.
Its beaches covered with thick tanker oil,
The sealife destroyed and its sky you spoil.
The beautiful beasts of the jungle are slayed,
For their ivory, skin, and coats displayed.
Slowly you cover each small piece of land,
With houses and factories - don't *you* understand?
That the more you take from this once lovely earth,
The less it can give as it loses its worth.
Slowly you kill it and all it contains,
Till only dry dust and ashes remain,
Look after it humans and like us give a cry,
But do something *we cannot* and don't let earth die!

B H Dance

CRIMES ON THE PLANET

From the beginning of time, God made the good things
Until man came along to destroy the planet and all that
                                        nature brings
God made everything, he divided the sea
Until man came along to ruin nature so free

From the beginning wild birds were tame
Even to the lion. Nature will never be the same.
Through years long past, there were horses and carts
The air which was breathed on was fresher in country parts.

Many of the crimes on this planet, I am going to mention
Is rubbish, filth, anything is thrown into seas causes pollution
Even to the lovely tree that brings life are cut down to nothing
Trees that lift each leafy arm in the spring.

Fumes from cars and lorries, doesn't help the fresh air.
Chemicals that are put in food isn't fresh like grandmas
                                        used to share
Leading to additive. A great deal is frozen
This could even be the cause of beef as it is now through
                                        the dozen.
                                                        Man

has destroyed the beauty on earth
Some folk are just for themselves, nothing for mirth
Rushing here, and rushing there
No time to look at nature fair.

Crimes, such things, get worse each year
On this planet which is spoilt, through to even fear
If we look at the balance, which man has destroyed, today
By just ruining the good things in life, that God made in His
                                        powerful way.

Jean P McGovern

46

MA'S PLACE

The greatest blunder of the
Universe,
Was not the explosion, that
Created Earth,

The elements, had made a big
Mistake,
One of, many things, was in the
wrong place,

Fish were alright, they had
their seas,
Animals survived, with a mixture of
Breeds,

Birds were guaranteed, a place
in the air,
The trees and flowers, had room
to spare,

Human beings, was the biggest
mistake,
They shouldn't be here, in this
Place,

The elements should have known,
from the start,
Humans always go back home,
to Mars.

John Burge

THE PERSONIFICATION OF MOTHER EARTH

Mother Earth is feeling sick.
We must do something very quick.
We bury our rubbish beneath her feet,
We are causing her to over heat.
It's not just because it's waste,
But the gases which it creates.

Hypothermia is what she's contracted,
From the way that we have all acted,
Her skirt of flowers and belt of leaves
Have got dry rot in the weave.
And as she ails with her back arched,
The land we till is looking parched.

We are even destroying her vital water,
Polluting our own food transporter.
Spewing toxins into an open sewer
Killing cod and the arctic skua.
All the wildlife will disappear,
As rot develops in her thermosphere.

Acid rain has begun to fall,
Killing some, but affecting all.
So as you lay soaking up the sun,
Just think back to what you have done.
It is us who have the upper hand,
So don't make this a desolate land.

Sharon Goodall

PURE, CLEAN AIR?

He gasps for breath
His body tired,
The pale, blue eyes beseeching,
Oh, will he die?
Hear Mother sigh
And prayers and love try reaching.

This child of life
Of tender years
Just five on his last birthday,
His wheezing rasp
A breath, a gasp
It's asthma draining life away.

Pollution black
Unseen grey air,
Choke airways of the young
The old so gasp
Car emissions pass
Asthma death, day has begun.

Clean air's a must
Speak out, let's fuss
Help man to be aware,
'Fore this people
All die gasping
We must have good, clean air!

Elizabeth M Sudder

THE END OF THE WORLD

As the lights go down
The windows close suddenly -
Everyone locks their doors.
Children hide under the covers,
While the God lovers begin to
Hold hands and pray:
Too late people
You're here to stay!

The fires are still burning -
Everything has turned to ash -
All you have to do
Is fight for your survival
No longer will there be guilty denial.

Money won't line your pockets
Just material possessions.
You have to travel on foot -
There is no fuel to drive a car.
Nothing has been left to survive.

Rich men won't eat gold coins -
They will eat the dirt on their faces -
The rest will follow on.
A poisonous island
Shall never regain its fertility.
There is no humility
Left in this place.

Savages are now apparent -
They have come from the Stone Age.
It will take a long time to rebuild this place -
Who will give a donation?
Oh Ram, why has it come to this stage!

Jagdeesh Sokhal

SAVE THEM

They're cutting, cutting, cutting everywhere
The tree's fast bucks to make
We've had enough, had our share
More than we can take.
Stop we say, and move on out
We'll give them all we've got
Let's be heard, let us shout
To stop this dirty rot
Gorillas, frightened under threat
Let's give them all we've got
We'll fight them in the woodland
The forest while they're there
Before they make them bare
The lion, hippo, birds and bees
The squirrel, fox the bear
Our friends, we'll save
To victory our flags we'll wave
For all life on earth we care.

Colin McCarthy

NO SUN IN THE SKY

Pollution on this planet is worsening by the day,
And soon it will get so bad that the sun will go away.
Floating fish and dying seals,
Means that we will have no meals,
Poisonous crops and poisonous air,
And yet manufacturers still don't care,
They don't realise that it is also their
children that could die,
Because of the pollution in the air and
no sun in the sky.

Emma Kemm

MAN'S INFIDELITY

If humanity evaluates life above all
Then the future of man is secure,
But if man over-values his worth above life
His self-destruction he will ensure.

Is it ego, or is it man's conviction
That he alone has a God-given right
To the exclusion and detriment of reason
Speeds ominously towards a perilous plight?

While man destroys his own environment,
Exterminates other life forms through greed,
Upsets mother nature's equilibrium,
Then his own demise is certain indeed.

William G Stannard

ECOLOGY

God furnished Noah with an ark
The purpose, survival, not extinction dark
Sixteen eighty! Dodo the last flightless birds
The buffalo, rhino and other *rapid fire herds.*

The red squirrel, cheetah, and the bat
Pandas, pine martins and the china tiger cat
We hunt for pelts, skins, and horn
But don't give time for new life to be born.

Plants, animals, reptiles die off as man fells trees
Birds become extinct, *what next bees?*
Corruption, greed , and yes, war
Why ruin this earth for evermore?

P Walker

GO GREEN FOR LIFE

Farmers of the world unite
Growing greens to win the fight
Everyone must try to endeavour
To balance out our stormy weather
The world could end in fiery flames
If we're not careful with our games
It's up to us 'cos we're to blame
Let's make things better and end our shame.

Gary Bradley

CALLING PLANET EARTH

There once was a world a long time ago
Where people lived and love did flow,
Mother nature was in her prime,
A happy place, a happy time.

But man decided he knew best
The earth felt the knife as it cut through her breast,
But man had power, the role of star player
There was suddenly a hole in the ozone layer.

People tried to warn them but
Man was oblivious, his eyes were shut,
And the little planet once so proud
Fell apart to a sobbing crowd,

Of course this story isn't all true
The end could be better, it's up to you,
We must do something now, it's time to act
Or it may come true and that's a fact.

Tracy Benjafield

MY NIGHTMARES
(Dedicated to Sylvia my wife, my life)

I am now past my three score and ten
Man has never really known peace, and I ask when
Even when my grandmother when she was old
Said I've never heard the bell of peace tolled
Even now I ask the same question *why*

Must this world always have wars, must we always suffer strife
I've not known peace in all my days and I've lived a long life
It's not plain and simple men, who starts these things
But politicians and various leaders who toll the bell for war to begin
It's just greed and power that these sort of men want

Why can't people be just like me
Happy content and carefree
A small garden to tend under a clear blue sky
And I often stop and look way up above way up high
If we continue on our way, destruction will come one day

The bombs man has made are so powerful
Countries and continents would just go out with a puff
Millions of people would disappear in a cloud of smoke
Why? Cannot man see he is heading towards doom
For when it's all over there will be plenty of room

But who wants to inherit a charred and blackened land
With no sign of any living thing
Those that survive, will not sing
For they will not have long to live
And for what some will say

I just hope that if they drop a bomb
Let it go off close to me
And blast me into eternity
Of one thing, I know at the end of my life
I can be reunited with my ethereal wife

Prince Rhan of Kathari

SHE WATCHES

The day is breaking into little bits
And she is no older
Than the rocks on which she sits,
Rocks which are stained
As she watches
The day like revolution has waned.

A fading sheet of black sky
Descends over the ocean and rocks,
She takes a handful of red sand from the hot clime
And slowly wonders why
The earth has to pay this time.

A fisherman sails out his steaming boat
But it will not stay afloat
And all the fish
Swim out of the sea,
The ocean's spirits has been drunk
Leaving a landscape of worthless junk.

Still she watches and follows the sky
Waiting for it to die,
And as the workers and miners are turned up
The day is torn into little strips
Another piece of green is cut away
Another person exits his stay.

James Norman

THIS WONDERFUL WORLD

God created the world in seven days,
If we read the Bible so it says,
Then He provided food for us to eat,
It really was a terrific feat!

Next, in His image He created man
And that's when His problems really began,
Because He gave man the gift of free will,
The ability to choose between good and ill.

Now man believes he's in charge of this planet
And doesn't need God's help to run it,
But 'global warming' and the 'greenhouse effect' are our lot
Making the temperature here on Earth so very hot.

Pollution too is a problem here,
Which is damaging the ozone layer.
Now is the time to stop and think
Before into total oblivion we sink.

We must find a way to protect our atmosphere
For it is a thing to us most dear.
We must save our planet from further harm
And save this world of beauty and charm.

Denise Harding

AN EARTHLY FAREWELL

They fell the trees, they dynamite the earth
the mighty caterpillar gorges for all its worth
without a care, without a damn
they prepare the great advance of man.

A surge forward into the jungle resplendent
hell bent for leather quite unrepentant
caring not that they upset the balance
of nature's age-old proven talents.

56

As Amazon trees are uprooted
entire communities are booted
trampling eco-systems of 'primitive' men
wiped out with the stroke of a pen.

Once more the greed of man
is destroying everything he can
as part of that historical story ever told
of man's evil intent to get his hands on gold.

John M O'Sullivan

MANIC DESTRUCTION

Man's progress planet earth has regressed
Violation of the land and sea repressed
The beauty and life the earth once bore
That we pitiful humans can never restore

Machines and technology have taken their toll
Life and work made easy for man
This so-called progress and knowledge
Has interfered with nature's balanced plan

Her trees and foliage have been replaced
Many of earth's creatures now displaced
Factories, towns and man-made dams
Have sprung up as if by magic to cover the land

Air that once was clean and sweet
Polluted by the vehicles that fill our streets
The water once so sparkling and pure
Filled with effluence teems with life no more

Even the sea that vast mysterious space
Cannot escape from pollution and nuclear waste
Instead of heeding the bright flashing signs
We carry on as usual - close our eyes to our crimes.

Elizabeth Amery

GUILTY NATION

Carbon monoxide fills the air,
Jog on the roads if you dare.
Guilty forest in an unkind world,
Tramps in cardboard city curled.

Set free is Nelson Mandella.
Edwina Currey said salmonella.
Sticker in a car window be
Shaped as petrol pump lead free.

Greenhouse effect on a blank screen
Everywhere's gone the colour green.
Chop, chop here, chop, chop there.
Could be a rainforest in despair.

A strike here a strike there.
More nuclear weapons prepare.
Inflation rising sky high
NHS oh goodbye, goodbye.

Acid parties in a warehouse.
The words Council Tax, what else!
The environment words to understand,
Oh, 'what have they done to our land!'

Irra Borthwick

DISGUST OF PITY

Pity the earth if you must pity dust -
The fallen continents cremated lie
And where the wave was wont to rage his lust
Is dull, unutterably dull, and dry.

Pity the sky, for so the habit grows
Out of one pity, pity those above:
The planets, stars and still unnumbered those
On whom your pity falls but not your love.

58

Oh, if you after all should pretext find
To pity any line, this hand that wrote,
Confine your pity to some other mind
Lost in its final emptiness to float.

Last, honest out of time, as ashes fall
Pity yourself, who devastated all.

Alasdair Aston

AN EPITAPH

Winding rivers, clean and clear
Wandered so for many a year,
Where trout and minnow, playful bream
Dart and twist with silver gleam.
Watercress and waving reed,
Verdant in sweet waters feed.
Moorhen glides with widening wake
Across a clear and crystal lake.
Sleek nourished kine dip at the brink
At eventide, so quiet to drink.
But soon these rivers thick with slime
Will wander for some future time,
Mirroring no more the blue blue sky,
Where fish choke and writhe and die,
And many plants which moisture seek
Are poor and sparse and struggling weak,
No more the birds, the banks along
Sing forth their joyous summer song,
And scraggy kine from drink recoil
From brinks lapped dark with snaky oil.
An epitaph for all mankind,
For space travellers some day to find
Here lies the foolish human race
Killed by progress's rapid pace.

James Barnwell

CONSCIENCE IN GOD'S WORLD

God gave the world a brand new start.
The global flood a work of art.
He cleansed the earth and made his mark.
For Noah and the famous ark.

If God could say some words to you.
About the earth right now.
I only know the words he'd say
Your conscience tells you how.

Did I ask you to destroy the earth for me.
Did you ask me, how I felt or feel.
Beg for forgiveness when all is wrong.
A beautiful gift destroyed nearly gone.

Pollution in the air you breath.
Pollution in the sea.
Pollution in the animals.
And in the greenery.

You bomb the land and in the sea.
And kill from hate inside.
The ice it melts so cold your hearts.
Destruction for you. Not me.

Just leave the earth alone right now.
As nature says. Let it be.
My gift is not for destroying.
But you will! Then where will you be.

Delline Docherty

SILENT MESSENGER

It stands, ice-bright
against the yielding landscape.
Government sold out to *energy efficiency:*
Micro chips, served on a plate.
The fate of *man*
buried in the bowels of Plutonium secrecy.
Cancer rods of iron
rule.
Pregnant with fear,
unwanted.
Birthed into life.
Pacified
with ministerial safety tours,
reports and balance sheets.
Once here, the *beast*
can never be ignored.
Cow's milk sparkles, fluorescent
in the glass.
Two-headed fish!
Better value than before
deformities entered the food chain;
causing Mad Cow disease
in the brain of *man.*
The *beast* spawned growth.
Not just monetary,
but cellular.
The silent stare of the feeders remain
ever hungry for space.
The silent scream screams on,
throat raw in irradiated pain.
Energy efficiency, and money
win the game.

Martina Peters

THE WORLD TODAY

The world is no longer pollution free,
Like years ago it used to be,
Fumes that make you cough and choke,
It isn't what you'd call a joke,
Rubbish is all dumped underground,
Methane gas may be leaked around,
Spraying is commonplace these days,
With it's drifting poisonous haze,
The water doesn't taste as seen,
Most likely, too much chlorine,
Now we've damaged the ozone layer,
And made a hole in the atmosphere,
Giant chimneys spread acid rain,
They try to clean it up in vain,
The nuclear threat hovers around,
One hopes a solution will be found,
Maybe one day, we'll learn the error of our ways,
And make this world a cleaner place,

Robert L Todd

CRIMES AGAINST THE PLANET

Our planet Earth used to be,
A thing of perfect beauty.
Birds would fly upon the wing,
Each breath of air was as fresh as spring.

But now that beauty has begun to fade,
And our planet is starting to decay,
With pollution in our oceans blue,
No longer are they safe for me and you.

62

Certain employers not giving a care,
They are not bothered for what is no longer there,
They are causing heaps of destruction,
For their so-called progress construction.

Manufacturers continue to sell,
Aerosol products that do so well,
Produce something safe that will help planet Earth,
Then you will realise what our planet is worth.

Mary Farr

HOW CIVILISED!

Ye banks and braes o' bonny doon,
Lie under lay-by north of Troon,
And Robert Browning's brushwood sheaf,
A transport cafe brought to grief

Where the bee sucks, there sucked I,
Until the Orbital came by,
And weeds along the motorway,
Were once the darling buds of May

While Wordsworth's host of daffodils,
Are killed by shovels, picks and drills,
'Loveliest of trees, the cherry now'
Is Chinese take-away in Slough

And where are Keats' moss'd cottage scenes?
A roundabout in Milton Keynes!
And silent is his woolly flock,
Beneath that shiny office block

On motorway, not country lanes,
I by-passed Newbury and Staines,
Good job in office, car I prized,
I smiled and thought - how civilised!

Dave E Priest

SICK SLICK

I hear that monstrous oil slick
reached the coastline that I love
and wonder
how could God above allow it?
The Pembrokeshire of my young days
is Dyfed now to many,
is it ever to be any more
unsullied?
It is a special place for me
a kind of peace hangs there
I cannot think of anywhere
I'd rather be - but now
it's safer to be far away.
To view the insidious oily streams
Sea Empress spewed
would shatter dreams
I treasure.
The patchwork hills remain the same
the farmhouses and mills
but sandy coves forever marred
by careless oil spills.
Don't show me pictures on TV
of distressed birds and seals
this only deals with here and now
what will tomorrow bring?
It may be wrong to criticise
I haven't seen with my own eyes,
I'll keep my memories as they were.
I would prefer it
that way.

Audrey Hardy

WALKING ON A TIGHTROPE

Our world is changing every day.
Life's precious forms along the way.
We hear about so many things,
Changing all that God brings.
Pollution is such an ugly word.
Aerosol and ozone are so often heard.
A World War has started without any guns.
While business men sit and do their sums.
Destroying our rain forests.
Destroying our lives.
Our hopes for the future,
We'll say our goodbyes.
Farm sprays, exhaust fumes and dumping waste.
Too many people not thinking, but doing in haste.
Our food is affected.
What is safe to eat?
There are problems with everything,
Especially the meat.
Mad Cow, Salmonella, on the menu today.
Should we listen to everything they have to say?
The fish they swim in polluted seas.
Deformed and affected soon to be.
When will we learn to change our lives?
The Government sits protected by walls.
Decisions it makes until it falls.
It's not too late to save our lands.
Let's all stand together and join our hands.
Recycle it. Save it and keep it green.
Think of the future.
Let's keep it clean!

Kay Johnson

SAVE OUR PLANET

There are many crimes against this planet earth
From the beginning of time, man's birth
The destruction a terrible disgrace
Nature ruined by the human race
Trees cut down for wood have gone
Rain forests where animals live and depend on
All this destroyed for our need
A selfish act of human greed
Cutting with the deadly chain-saw
For furniture houses and more
Pollution from chemicals in the air
Human beings they don't care
Tourists collect and destroy coral reefs
An underwater wasteland, it's beyond belief
Dams, and flooding of forest land
Why spoil this place so grand?
When I think what man's done I fear
All these creatures and habitats may disappear
Deforestation will change our weather, we'll find
A true disaster for all mankind.

K Brown

OUR WORLD TODAY

Concrete and tarmac all over the place
No room for bushes or trees
Cows in stalls, pigs in pens
And sewage dumped out in the seas

Fumes from vehicles spoil the air
Invading the lungs of us all
Sometimes sitting over the city
A deadly thick grey pall

The people in charge don't seem to care
They encourage all this pollution
By cutting trees and building roads
They won't hear a simple solution

If only someone would see sense
Get rid of the motor car
We'll all use buses, bikes or walk
And enjoy our cleaner air.

R A Quinney

OUR SO-CALLED 'LESSER BRETHREN'

What dreaded pollution is an oily slick
When birds' feathers become a deadly wick?
Dying birds; disabled birds suffer on the sand,
Never more to fly free above the sea and land.

We should all care and bear responsibility,
For all the pollution we create,
Like thick green scabs of lichen,
That grow and float heedless on the lakes.

Do wildlife on land or fish in the sea,
Cause mayhem, filth and odour with impunity?
These our so-called lesser brethren,
That many would have us believe,
Live their lives according to God's laws,
The way it was meant to be.

We pollute the atmosphere, rivers and seas,
We make acid rain that falls silently on trees.
If only we were as *dumb* as the creatures
Beneath our poisonous thumb,
There'd be no more smog; no more waste,
And there'd be no more pollution.

Mavis Hardy

HOPE FOR TOMORROW

Wars have been declared
And some ran scared
Into the deep recesses of their mind
Especially when they did not want to end up blind

Some relish the thought of killing
But for me it's far too chilling
There is nothing noble in dying
Especially when the rulers are lying

For what does it gain a man
To lay down his life for something they should ban?
There is nothing honourable about death
Especially when they bury you six feet beneath

Never deceive yourself or others
If war comes remember the suffering mothers
They have to endure heartache
Especially just because of someone's hearsay

Rise up and oppose tyranny in any form
If you really want to be re-born
Remember if you take the Queen's shilling
Then you are only too willing
Especially to continue the killing.

Alastair Buchanan

CRIMES OF TODAY

If there wasn't much up in space,
Perhaps it would be a better place,
And of course for the human race.

All these things like satellites you see,
In summer it's making it hot which,
Isn't how it used to be.

It doesn't matter about our creed or colour
What about the air we breathe?
It's not as clean as it was years ago
Perhaps these things are now about to show.

Then there's the pollution that's killing
our birds,
Surely this is so absurd?

Nicola Regan

LOOK WHAT YOU'RE DOING

Look what you're doing against old Mother Earth.
Pollution from cars.
Pollutions from spilt oil.
Not only are you ruining the air you're ruining the soil.

Look what you're doing can't you see the destruction
The CFC's
The oil pollution and the gases destroying the ozone layer.
This isn't fair.

Soon if nothing is done
We won't have any earth to live in.
Get your facts right.
All this destruction must be a sin.

Look what you're doing
Dumping all the sewage into the sea.
Can't you see what you're doing
Soon there won't be any earth left not only for our children's
children,
But for you and me.

James R B McCurdie

TRAFFIC

Early morn
Blaring horn
Traffic light
Road rage fight.

Heavy lorries
Leaving quarries
Block the motorway
Every single day.

Traffic zooms
Toxic fumes
Cause pollution
No solution.

More roads
Increasing loads
Take the bend
Where will it end?

Angela Ballester

IRONY

You smoke, you smoke, you terrible bloke.
You're polluting the planet and me,
And there on the track, he ate his Big Mac
And threw the box under a tree.

His unruly hound found a spot on the ground
And of nature, obeyed the call.
Then to my dismay, a child at his play,
Into the pile did fall.

The lad, when he stood, did all that he could
To wipe his hands clean and dry:
And as I looked again, I watched in cold pain,
As the lad wiped a tear from his eye.

I started to speak, to tell him what cheek,
That he should accuse me so,
But with a clatter and clang, he threw down his
beer can,
And turned on his heel to go.

Billy Baird

THE NIGHT SKY

Still darkness of the night
When sky dawns her black evening gown
Aglow like diamonds the stars sparkle
I think of folks in city streets
Who see little of the sky
Their view is the fairy lights that shine
From towering blocks on high
When I look through my window
Oh lucky, lucky me, I see the cattle
Sheltering 'neath the weeping willow tree.

There in God's vast mantle above
God controls universal domain
Moon by night man shall not smile
Nor yet the sun by day.

Man's made a mess of earth and sea
Cruelty pollution continually
Man on the moon, yes we did see.
To inhabit the moon, God says
'No! That cannot cannot be.'

Frances Gibson

CRIMES AGAINST THE PLANET

There is so much pollution because of so many cars
People using aerosols with CFCs in
The destruction of this planet has become a crime
Crimes against the planet are caused every time
So many people pollute this planet, factories' smoke up into the air
For these things are crimes against the planet.

God created this planet then along came man
Trees being cut down to suit man
People aren't bothered about the destruction
No-one seems to be bothered that because
Trees are cut down, animals and birds are losing their homes
For man started to destroy the balance and committed some awful crimes
For these are crimes against the planet.

Geraldine Perkins

THE ROAD TO DESTRUCTION

Unknown forces are always at work
Tampering with planet Earth's core,
Volcanoes, floods and swelling oceans
Earthquakes, disease and war.
Now there is a hole in the roof of the world
Because of toxic emissions,
How much more punishment can it take
Before it's too late for decisions?
Leave the rain forests to carry on growing
Stop interfering with nature,
Allow an interval of time to heal
Give children a decent future.
The Twentieth Century has a lot to answer for
Because of modern methods of construction,
Too much technology has guaranteed
That we are on the road to destruction.

Patricia Frampton

POLLUTION SOLUTION

It seems to be the aim of man
to spread disaster as far as he can
instead of taking care of the planet
doing everything he can to destroy it.

From chemical waste to nuclear dumping
from deforestation to oil slick pumping
into the oceans and onto the land
pollution has raised a deadly hand.

The ozone layer is thinning out
because motor car rules and runs about
ever increasing in numbers and size
making clean air a treasured prize.

Now this madness has to stop
and global warming has to drop
combustion engines will have to go
or else man will be his own worst foe.

If this remedy proves too late
- the horse has gone, we shut the gate;
then our legacy to our young
will be regret at the chance we flung

away and watch ten thousand years
could prove the worst of all our fears
and the twentieth century could be
the last of running wild and free.

So let there be a world think-pound
where problems are shared and solutions found
where differences are put aside at last
and pollution made a thing of the past.

David Robb

WHEN WILL?

When will the time come for the death of sin?
When will the crooked man lose his crooked grin?
When will a baby breathe unpolluted air?
When will life be justified, strong enough to care?

When will fear of war cease to exist?
When will love step in to assist?
When will pipes of freedom echo through the land?
When will persecution be forever banned?

When will the rebels take heed of the rules?
When will we put an end to trigger-happy fools?
When will law and order hold its head up high?
When will tears of innocence stop trickling from our eye?

When will all the nations unite to form a band?
When will children run and play safely in the sand?
When will conservation open up the door?
When will murky waters stop drifting to the shore?

How many years will it take to set a blind man free?
How many years will it take before we all can see?
Everything around us is turning into dust
Mighty be the sword of death that makes the final
Thrust!

David P Elliott

SADDAM AND TOMORROW

When the desert turned black it wasn't the sky
that reflected the dark-skinned beauty on high.
When the desert turned black it wasn't a storm
that kissed our skin as we sweated so warm.
When the desert turned black it shattered us all
as we gazed at a planet sticky with oil.

But when the sand turned to flame Armageddon had come
to burn and to poison us all 'til there was none.
Deep pools of crude so vile and so rude
so inhuman, this incomprehensible flood.
An act so obscene it defies all belief
all we can do in our misery and grief
is pray that our children will learn form the past
and never forget that day the sand turned to glass.

B Wood

HAS GOD FORGOTTEN THE POOR?

God has provided for the poor
By giving us that much more.
How to share, how to give.
Difficult indeed, to send to those in need.

Eat tea while watching telly,
See the child with swollen belly.
Does it move us to send some money,
Or are we too busy feasting on honey?

Kurds, Indians, and Africans too;
Lay dying - in need of me, in need of you.
God forgive the hand that will not share,
God forgive those who do not care.

Suffering and poverty everywhere.
Famines, floods and disasters are rife,
Thousands of people deprived of life.
Sick of seeing? Smash the screen!
Don't want to hear? Block an ear!

For there are no prizes for wanting to share.
God has provided for the poor,
By giving us that much more!

Neville Hawkins

75

OUR POISONED PLANET

Tuned to perfect harmony,
That's how nature used to be.
That was when the world began,
Before the interference of man.

The sun has become our enemy,
Giving off rays we cannot see.
The ozone layer has many holes,
Causing malignant tumours and moles.

Native habitats are destroyed every day,
When acres of rain forest are hacked away.
The balance of nature is turned around,
And climatic changes are profound.

Nuclear waste is here to stay,
There is no way it can go away.
Imported from across the world so wide,
Transported across our countryside.

Toxic waste is dumped at sea,
Swimming can a health risk be.
Untreated sewage invades the beaches,
Along with oil from tankers' breaches.

Exhaust fumes form traffic pollute the air,
Children with asthma are seen everywhere.
Juggernauts thunder down most of our roads,
Shattering eardrums and shaking abodes.

Our fruit and vegetables we must wash well,
Pesticides may be present, we cannot tell.
There is also danger in our water and meat,
But what can we do? We must drink and eat!

A A Hargreaves

MANKIND

The entry of man within this earth,
The way we created and the way we gave birth
Have slowly polluted this place we call home,
This space on earth we call our own.
The ozone layer is messed up, the hole is growing fast,
This destruction of the earth how long will it last?
They're destroying all the trees, they'll worry later,
We need trees to live, and them, they wanna make paper.
Well that now I can believe.
Soon, we'll be paying for the air that we breathe,
People scared to go out thro' anger and fear,
The crime population grows every year.
Someone must be doing something wrong,
About this I could probably write a song.
But seriously something needs to be done
With these different rules for everyone.
Then slowly but surely we turn into a living concrete.

Kieghley Joyce

THE HUMAN SPECIES

A parsnip nose on a turnip head
Hollow eyes coloured black and green
A knife sharp slit of a turned down mouth
This robot face you oft' have seen.

For we're all made the same of mud and clay
Out of God's hands like the bird and tree
We're brash, we're trash, we're just mere ash
But we're special, we are, just you and me!

Mary Hayworth

77

THE DESTROYER

The drifting, choking dust,
And flesh-stinging grit,
Needling my body as I sit -
So weak, that sit I must.
The clothing I have left
Will not cover up my head;
I could not steal from the dead,
Or even crawl to make a theft.
Beside me a small grave,
A passing soldier's enforced seed;
Other deaths in memory plead,
Five more I failed to save.
Once I dreamt of mealie meal,
Perhaps a little oil . . .
Vegetables from our rich soil.
But hunger I no longer feel.
When northern rains fail,
The refugees southward swarm,
Sparking military storm,
Resistance is of no avail.
I am so dust surrounded,
None will find me here,
Dying with a dreadful fear
My loss will be compounded.
Breathing a prayer whilst I can
'God protect Africa
Against that vile trafficker
Profligate, uncaring *man*.'

Di Bagshawe

LOW SOCIETY

Does nobody care about this world of ours
The ruin, decay, misery?
The sad faces of people who feel they've no hope
Does nobody see?

Does nobody care for the plight of the young
When their schools fall apart at the seams,
With no jobs to be had and nowhere to have fun,
Can nobody see?

Does nobody care if there are no homes
For the people asleep on the streets
With no place to go to and no-one to love,
Will nobody see?

Does nobody care if the hospitals close
Leaving nowhere for those who are weak
And the old and the sick have to suffer alone,
Do they not want to see?

Does nobody care about those who are starving
As they carve a slice of their meat,
Or the wells that are dry and the crops that have died
When will someone see?

Does nobody care as they pickup their axe
To cut down the very last tree
That they bring self-destruction, and then it's too late
They'll wish they had seen . . .

Mary Brooke

CRIMES AGAINST THE PLANET

God created planet Earth
and all living beings
To live in peace and harmony
with us as humans

But we chose our own ways
of a life in killing
Following our evil desires
without any feeling

Creatures, great and small
have turned against our will
All over the communities
most people are becoming ill

War is *man's* greatest destruction
destroying food and homes
The awful tension of isolation
for all who are lame and without limbs

We sin against our bodies
we sin against our minds
we sin against each other
it's worse than going blind

No-one knows for sure
what will happen after
But be warned there's a burning fire
of hell waiting for us somewhere . . .

Jenny Cheung

BITTER PILL

'The poor Earth she is choking,
and scarred beyond belief'
said the Lord to all the Chosen,
and even to the thief.
Spinning in the darkness, creation's greatest jewel,
slowly devastated by this thing called *man,*
a simple, clever being, but nonetheless a fool.
With toxins, dioxins, radiation and man-made plague,
little decent land left, to dig the dead their graves.
All of us are guilty, no need to blame those past,
such intelligence, destruction by atomic blast.
Is there anything that we can do, atone for all our crimes?
And put right all the damage, inflicted by mankind.
I do not know the answers, and probably never will,
but don't let the Earth die screaming,
the result of a swallowed, bitter pill.

Pat Judson

A CRAZY WORLD

We live in hatred enmity and strife
People of our planet wage cruel wars
Make a desert of earth, destroying life
Not too late, to seek the cause
Pollution of oceans land atmosphere
Devastation of our planet will appear
Erasing life plus the human race
Greed, arrogance, egoism and evil.
A planet, blanketed with radiation
It's the way of the devil
Not the way to salvation.

Richard Lloyd

PLASTICITY

The army was advancing on the scientist in his lair
Horizon was pulsating with numbers . . . (count who'd dare?)
He quickly climbed the stairway to lock himself away
He could not face the enemy or hold them far at bay
Out front they had a leader, swaying, plunging forth
The army spread behind him, from east, west, south and north . . .
He trembled in his prison watching the advance
An army huge and powerful, not even there by chance
He knew there was no answer, to stop them 'twas too late
Creating such a mass of waste had led them to this fate,
Bottles, sacks, containers, huge pipes and building stock
All items made in plastic, never ending waste en block
Mankind was the developer, they thought that they were king
Now they were to be vanquished by a plastic army ring . . .

Margarette L Damsell

FRIENDS OF THE EARTH?

Slowly, I walk along this simple golden beach . . .
Descriptions of the beauty of nature, I beseech . . .
Watch waves roll and crash against the sandy shore . . .
Amid all this sublime beauty, from reality I'm tore . . .
Yet as I stumble along the sand, a discovery I make . . .
A sewage pipe, forcing waste to the sea, in a polluted lake . . .
What is this, I'm disgusted by this horror that faces me . . .
So much, Homo sapien defecation pumped into the sea . . .
And yet further along the sand, I see children stray . . .
Playing in the water, I fear the filth floats their way . . .
So I question the morals, of those dwelling upon the earth . . .
Have they no concept of the ocean's great worth . . .
That they would pollute the ocean, where their children play . . .
I am so disgusted, I turn and walk away . . .

John Graham

A THOUGHT AND A PRAYER

The land so bare and desolate the
world has been at war striking with
such force no-one has ever seen before.

With all their power and weaponry
and their greed and lust these
people we call leaders have reduced
our world to dust.

Just a broken empty shell left to
float around in space. No longer to
exist as God's created human race.

So please dear Lord up above who
rules this planet Earth we love, help
us all to live in peace before we
all become deceased.

For it won't be long before mankind
destroys this world of yours and
mine, so help us now while there's
still time.

Ernest Hiddleston

VERDICT

People cry as forests die,
they fall without rhyme or reason,
empty spaces filled with grass
lend weight to human treason.

The arguments are trotted out,
the familiar words are said,
leaving man alive yet wrong
and nature right but dead.

Mark Morris

PARADOX

They snake across the country,
Concrete, tarmac, narrow or wide
Carrying the nation's life blood
From towns to country side.
These lanes, roads, motorways,
Transporting our necessities
To every corner of the land
Supporting our economies.
We make more highways,
We have too many cars,
But to keep our industry
We produce without cares.
They pour along ceaselessly
Red, black, green, and blue
Bellowing, noxious, choking,
Deadly exhaust fumes to spew.
Trees we need to give us air,
We rip them from the ground,
To make way for more lorries
Our lovely land to pound.
It's strange on what we rely
Hastens on our own deaths.
A sad fact we can't deny
We are robbing our own breath.

Raymond J Lewis

84

A LOOK THROUGH ALL THE EYES

Looking at the village site again
I contemplate my shadow
upon the rock's shadow where I sit.
People are so pathetically
temporary and fragile.
Our dreams give a glimpse
finding oneself
on an unmarked path
walking over a breakable globe
amble towards a planet
space-scape for humans.
In black and white
in red and yellow
our work became tight, ie,
the freest gift:
map and key:
drawing, outline, impulses
and tragedy.
Everywhere we are flawed and horrible;
there are those who dress,
refine and defend the crimes
and horrors of wars.
We wear greater tragedy!
'In nature there are no countries'
as Gary Snyder says.
In countries there are no states,
provinces and national boundaries.
This planet is a *verb*
a celebration of a whole species
in *freedom and love.*

Daniel De Culla

ATTRACTIONS VERSUS FORCE

When God started making things, what did He do?
Made it all out of nothing (you know this is true!)
No physical arms, or, legs did He need,
Just the art or attraction performing each deed!
Even Adam and Eve had the power to attract,
God never forced them to do any act!
But - men started ruling men by brute force
Till the art of attraction was very near lost!
You see: force is man's way: attraction is not!
And anything gained by sheer force will just rot!
So, to keep love alive, keep attracting your mate!
Never bully or pester! Be patient and wait!
Or, like seeds that are forced to grow fast overnight,
Love will curl up and die in a terrible fright!
Let them do things their way; say nothing, or, praise
When they make a mistake, a kind word always pays!
Just being thought *great* is all they need to know!
If you cover their errors, your own may not show!
Use attraction always, gentle, pure as a dove -
Just a smile and a hug and *let go* - that's love!

Catherine Flint

PAPER

If I were into stocks and shares, I think the ones I'd buy
Would be to do with paper, for, no matter how I try
I can't avoid the use of it, nor stop it coming in.
Its all-pervading presence seems to me an awful sin.

There's folk whose land is dying, for their trees are being cut:
No roots to hold the soil in place, no shade nor shelter, but
It seems we cannot do without our paper nowadays.
I wonder how we did before - there must be other ways.

86

Agreed, we need a little bit to see us all get through,
But what concerns me is the waste. One day we'll surely rue
The devastation to our world, the thoughtlessness and greed.
Is it too late to use just what we do not want, but need?

I could, or should have written this on skin, or leaves on bark,
But habits are so hard to break, and one must make one's mark.
I could have used my memory and only once have writ.
I'm guilty, like the rest of us: *I've hyperpapered it!*

Moira Vaughan

DEAR CREATOR . . .

In ignorance we strive to copy Thee.
To call this world our own.
The lakes, which only You can fill.
The trees, Your breath has grown.
We say 'Of God there is no sign'
Yet puzzlement abounds.
What was it gave the eagle flight,
The nightingale her sound?
What is it makes the winds to blow,
And mighty oceans roar?
Yet calms and stills my storm-filled mind
And urges, 'Try once more.'
When hopelessness would drag me down
What hand supports my walk?
What lifts me high on eagles' wings
And strengthens my weak flight? . . .

. . . A cross, a tomb, - an *empty* grave.
Tools He used, to give my eyes new sight
And life, that I with Him should *live,*
And daily give to Him the glory that is His by right.

Christina Fowler

A SHORT STORY ABOUT THE DEATH OF A VILLAGE

my village is behind me
breathing for the last time
since dawn i have waited
now the sun is hot
it shimmers nervously
anticipating commercial sponsorship
an electricity company or so i've been told

soon the dam slams shut
and where i sit will be drowned
the life blood turned killer
filling the sky with a constant thunder
as the turbines whirr
promising abundance
i'm told to be happy

you can use tv's
and washing machines
and computers
but they're swimming out of reach
the land has been stolen
my family evicted
our history ignored

that is what they tell me

so i shall not smile
i shall not move

Stuart Meacham

CAR OR CANCER

Dust from its rubber tyres on wheels of four,
From the car's exhaust oily smoke it pours;
A bluish black plume, these fumes we consume,
With cancer we die,
We wonder why.

With money and science they search for a cure,
But they will not find it, that's for sure,
As long as we want our cars today,
This plague of cancer will not go away.

So rid of this oil and rubber
And clean air we must recover,
If we want our next generation to survive,
Do away with this polluted vehicle,
While we are still alive.

George S H Seymour

LISTEN!

They'll listen now; wait and see
they'll know I'm right; look to me
it's not too late; to save the day
we have to do it; do it this way
choking the sky; poisoning the soil
ways we can combat; ways we can foil
out in the ocean; under the sea
work as a team; I think you'll agree
it's up to us; to put things right
throw down the challenge; take up the fight
this earth is ours; it's not too late
can't leave it to chance; mustn't leave it to fate!

Mike Perrett

AN ECLIPSE OF AN APOCALYPSE

With the soil plagued
Where once the feathered
For flight feed treads
Mother Nature's greatest rapist
Whose now even demons migrate,
All in awe, dreading the hot
Hive that is global, and desert
Bound and cast are his guardian angels.

Smouldering paths, burnt stone
And cracked are the charcoal
Highways, while mysterious potions
Swarm the oceans making sick
The seven seas, all are
Witness to this, even war pestilence
Hunger and disease.

Gerry McAleney

GREENPIECE

The human race has done great harm
To hedgerow, millpond, moor and farm.
New pesticides and harmful spray
On apples, berries, veg and hay
May bring mutations, pain, disease
Less honey from the bees, no trees.
Before the greenhouse gets too hot
Let's stop this universal rot;
Ban pesticides for our own good
And only eat organic food.

Mary Rea

CRIME

Pressures occurring,
Hell breaks loose,
My life shatters,
Black and white is all I see,
My heart bleeds,
My body aches,
My soul cries,
The world is an evil place,
I wish I had not matured,
I wish I were a child,
With no conscience,
Hurt and betrayed,
Life's not as innocent as I thought,
Life is evil,
This planet is sheltered with crime.

Shazia Afzal

PLANET EARTH - PART 3

Pressure those uncontrollable gases escape.
Atmosphere choking in their wake.
Small unborn children are distressed,
Their mothers choking for another cigarette.

What was not before is here with us now,
Clinging to everything and snarling all up.
Chemicals used in the battle to cleanse.
Adding still more to this pointless mess.

As there are those who still dream,
Of a planet pure and clear.
But thousands of years will elapse of doom.
Our prehistoric self will be for insects to gaze.

Marcus Fyfeldi

91

MEARE HEATH, SOMERSET LEVELS

Grotesque,
Slag-heapesque
Peat, piled high.
Dark mound,
Squelching ground,
Blacked-out sky.

Birds call?
Not at all;
Plants gone too.
Bare earth;
No spring birth;
Nothing new.

Bleak scene,
Stagnant rhyne;
Caravan
In bits;
Rubbish tips.
Curséd man!

Pat Moore

SUNSET

The golden sun's fast sinking rays,
Mark the closing of another day,
Before the dark night skies appear,
We come to God and humbly pray,
For peace on earth and wars to cease,
And bitter hate to turn to love,
So that this green and pleasant earth
May resemble heaven's courts above.

G A Burgess

THE FALL OF MR AXE

There was a man called Mr Axe;
He had no conscience, ignored facts.
He cut down forests for his food,
And left the landscape bare and rude.
He was well paid and lived in style,
With houses, cars, with girls who smile.
But then *catastrophe* appeared;
A hurricane with wild winds steered
Into the courtyard of his dreams,
And burst through every structure's seams.
It swept away all in its path;
There was no insect left to laugh.
Trees which had given fruit and nut
Could not provide, they'd all been cut.
No wood for shelter, all the land
Had nothing left but dust and sand.
And Mr Axe cursed all his greed
Which now could not produce one feed.
He had not listened to wise folk
Who'd said, 'Replant with every stroke.'
The artefacts of Man were stilled
As Mr Axe fell down, self killed.
He groaned and uttered one last sigh;
'The greed that filled has made me die.'
The death of Man had come too soon;
Wisdom too weak to kill the *goon*.

J P C Ludford

SKY BLUES

Sky over Istanbul is yellow like a bruise
And air three-quarters ash.
I saw no dolphins on my pleasure cruise:
The waves disgorged a rigmarole of trash.

The world's a ball, and what a ball we've made it!
God gave it us in trust - and we betrayed it.

Chernobyl fall-out flutters in the breeze
And Europe's forests wilt in acid rain;
The prions of Mad Cow Disease
Can stipple and unhinge the human brain.

Three-score and ten is our allotted span:
A little less if we enjoy a tan.

Le smog in Paris chokes you as you 'stroll':
The city life our planet can't sustain.
As Athens stifles in its airless bowl
So all our futures spiral down the drain.

Earth is an apple and ourselves the worm:
Close up the school-room, it's the end of term.

Brian Poole

MOTHER EARTH

Where snow-capped mountains touch the sky
Rivers run deep, and the eagles fly.
Forests of pine roll down to the sea
The wind carries dreams to their destiny.

Where badger and bear roam free at night
Shimmering stars fill the shadows with light
Dolphins leap from an ocean blue
Clouds on fire in a sunset hue.

Where swirling mists greet a summer's dawn
Nature unwraps new sculptures born.
Valleys so deep, with colours in shade
Flowers so delicate, their beauty displayed.

Where unspoilt landscapes cry to be seen
A gentle breeze so fresh and clean
Bleached white sands, awash with foam
      Wonders abound
      Mother earth we call home . . .

T Hannah (GIG)

UNTITLED

I haven't got long left on the earth
I'll tell you my story for what it's worth
Yesterday I was fluffy and white
But at the moment I look a sight
For I was with friends swimming the seas
Splashing and playing all at ease
The sun was bright the sea was clear
Then a tanker spilt oil here
I've been pushed on the rocks
I have no defence
As oil seeps my body
I'm losing my strength
I've tried to fly to no avail
I feel I'm the weight of a whale
My feathers are stuck like glue to my side
There's my friend washed up by the tide
My breathing is short
I'm finding it hard
As oil poisons my body
Lights become dark.

Joe Proc

THE CONCRETE JUNGLE

Here in the concrete jungle, we have all we need
Free from the restrictions of nature, we alone succeed
Down in the concrete jungle, we make all the rules
Free from our responsibilities to nature, we can act like fools
Here in the the concrete jungle, we alone are king
Believing in our power of nature - we can do anything
Down in the concrete jungle, power is our goal
Ignoring the balance of nature - we gladly sell our soul

Here in the concrete jungle, we ruthlessly expand
We destroy the beauty of nature to satisfy our demand
Down in the concrete jungle, we never think twice
Rejecting the warnings of nature, we don't need advice
Here in the concrete jungle, we take, but we don't give
Abusing the laws of nature, that's the way we live

Violence! Pollution! Deprivation! Destitution!
Cruelty! Persecution! Corruption! Absolution!
Radiation! Deforestation! Exploitation! Starvation!
Hatred! Degradation! Intolerance! Indignation!

Down in the concrete jungle, power is our goal
Ignoring the balance of nature - we gladly sell our soul
Here in the concrete jungle, we take, but we don't give
Abusing the laws of nature, that's the way we live

Terry Bamforth

WATER FOR LIFE

Without water there is no life,
Yet there is trouble and strife.
We need oxygen and water to live,
Oxygen is freely available to give,
To us the power to breath in the air.
Water is for drinking and our bodily care.
You'd think we'd be very grateful,
Instead we are extremely hateful.
Always craving for the ultimate desire,
Never satisfied with what we acquire.
The best things in life are free,
And all around for us to see.
The sun by day and the moon by night,
To lighten our day, and at evening moonlight.
Nature's wildlife and the countryside,
Should be enough to fill us with pride.
But money position power and greed,
Overwhelm our normal basic need.
There is no limit to our aspirations,
So we are not content with admirations.
We destroy all that we hold dear,
Even turning water into beer,
Whisky spirits wines and cider.
We even shoot the lovely tiger.
Jungles and wildlife disappear,
And no-one seems to shed a tear.
We explode nuclear bombs beneath the sea,
Harming the coral reefs and humanity.
Will we never ever learn
To respect instead of spurn?

Brian Watson

SKIN TRADE

Out of the gibbering night three little men,
silent and deft, set up their tiger snare,
squatted near to wait, rolled cigarettes.
I think I thought: if tiger furs provide
food for their sickly little kids . . . well then . . . ?
And such a great beast, such little men . . .
But then the tiger came, parting the darknesses,
to fall spitting, snarling, awkward in their wires;
and though they'd killed him, a long and furious hiss
of rage and teeth and blood and dying fires
made them pause. Unmoved, they smoked until he lay
still, heavy, dead and safe. They cut the nets
and then, quickly and quietly they began to flay.
Well, then I wished, their engineering having gone amiss,
that he had reached them with a tiger's kiss.

They worked with little scraps of razor blades,
beginning with the soft, gold underbelly hair.
'Oh no!' I cried aloud. 'No! Don't start there.'
But TV is the past. Tigers are dead,
the real crooks never show; they wait elsewhere . . .
Yet it was still from these humanity had fled.
The rolled up beauty, their commission done,
was stuffed in plastic bags, and they were gone.

Patience Tuckwell

A GOWER JOURNEY

From Head of Worm to Mouth of Oyster,
Splendid majesty prevails;
Where yellow rock meets azure sea,
Mighty waves devour sails.

Leave Evans' church and venture east,
Past Mewslade, on to Thurba Head;
To Deborah's Hole and Paviland,
Where is the lady painted red?

Turn inland to Pitton Cross,
For a lazy ride on Tucker's mare;
Back to the coast, past nature's grandeur,
Approaching Culver Hole with care.

The golden sands and gentle waves
Appear serene and tame;
Who can forget poor Ivanhoe,
Her Master thought the same.

To Oxwich Point, with views supreme,
What better place to spend a day;
Across the Pill at Nicholaston,
The jagged teeth of Three Cliffs Bay.

Moving on to Minchin Hole,
With dark imposing porch;
Check the tide, two hours to spare,
Did we bring the torch?

Still perfect coast, but winter only
To avoid the grockle horde;
Past Caswell, Langland and Mumbles Pier,
To the castle's verdant sward.

Gower's coastline reigns supreme,
Just close your eyes and dream and dream . . .

Peter Towndrow

FROGS' LEGS

Jeremy Fisher had it easy.
Swallowed by a trout
And then spat out,
All he lost were his galoshes.

Not for him
The razor thin
Knife blade
Stuck up from the ground
So the handler,
In two swift movements
Can slice the kicking,
Thrusting, vital limbs
From the body;
A body then tossed aside
Onto a heap of
Writhing, bleeding amphibia,
Doomed to a lingering death
In confused agony.

Flies descend
And start their flesh-eating ritual
Round open wounds;
Flies no longer threatened
By dazed half frogs.

Seated on the ground,
A dozen women peel off
The skin from each
Mouth-watering leg,
Oblivious, numbed by their task.
Skins one way, legs another;
Packed away in ice.

A hundred million frogs
Cruelly slaughtered for dinner.
A thousand mouths await
The sensation of
This gourmet's delicacy.

Geoff Owen

GOODBYE TO EARTH

Goodbye to Earth,
I loved you well,
but I must leave you now.
Goodbye sun, rain,
moon, stars,
countryside I love,
the shore I love more.
Farewell to men,
their threats, our ruin,
little gods who are just men.
There may be a better place,
but Earth is perfect,
while men sleep,
their minds quiet,
their hands still,
their dreams of wealth,
only dreams.
Goodbye to Earth,
for now you pay man's price,
but dreams turn,
so to all you left behind,
learn to love your Earth.

H R Burns

SHE NEEDS A DOCTOR

The Earth has feelings as well
Which any bright person can tell
She needs a doctor to heal her scars
She needs a mechanic to demolish all cars
We all are lodgers in the Earth's own house
We are all equal from a snake to a mouse
We hold the knives which stab her in the heart
Don't deny it as we all take part
In killing this Earth
Making her weak
Her chances of living are looking so bleak
We have to change our ways
If she is to survive
Clean up our acts if she's to stay alive
Without our Earth we all would die
Then it will be too late to try
To bandage these wounds of this fatal war
Come on people we must try some more.

Donna Cass (15)

THE DESTROYER

At Moonfleet, where in days gone by
The pirates landed contraband
And fought with revenuers who
Were brave enough to make a stand

We picked up conkers in the woods,
Picked primroses along the banks
Of ditches and found violets
Which had escaped the tracks of tanks

That trained there before going off
To war. So much of beauty still
Beneath these quiet trees. And men
Have fought their war, and won, but now

The battle's just begun between
Nature and modern farmers' aids;
New chemicals more lethal far
Than were the ancient pirates' raids.

Dorothy Davis-Sellick

RULERS OF THE WORLD

Rulers of the world who live in the clouds
Ignore problems that abound on the ground
And like ostriches their heads in the sand
They too will soon be buried under the ground
The tenancy for mankind upon this planet is so short
We depart before we can be taught
And like all life upon this planet must
Return from whence they came into the dust
Lessons from the past return
Seems mankind will never learn
Take care mankind the actions you pursue
Lest the prophecy that mankind will destroy
Himself will soon come true.
Is it too much to ask the leaders of the world to unite
And find the solutions for the problems for all mankind
Surely we could build a heaven wherein we dwell
Instead of the actions taken that make a hell?

H R Coupe

MOTH NOTHINGNESS

Once in Britain, there were over seven
hundred different moth species, many
creatures of great interest and beauty.
Equally important, moths and their larval stages
formed a staple diet of several amphibians,
reptiles, birds and small mammals.

Before the last war, moths were abundant, regularly seen;
adults, drawn to lights, often came into villas on dark nights
through open doors or windows, clustered fluttering,
numerous as summer snowflakes, in car headlight beams;
their milliard caterpillars crawled over everything.

This no longer is the case; moths have become a rarity, it seems,
and butterflies, though only seventy species, far more common.
What's the reason moths are now so few in any season?

Most moths fly at night, are then strongly drawn to lights.
During the war, the countryside was dark at night
but ever since, the sky has been awash with light;
powerful moth-attracting lamps glare almost everywhere,
likely to interfere with their breeding behaviour.

Males detect mates by way of pheromones -
chemical scents to which they are very sensitive and home in on,
while female moths in similar vein often find thereby
specific caterpillar food-plant egg-laying sites.
Many of their requisite food-plant habitats have been quite widely
destroyed by farming and development, and extraneous
chemical environmental pollutants in variety
may interfere with mating and egg-laying, for
moths and larvae are killed by insecticides,
their food-plants sometimes removed by herbicides.

As a consequence, this moth nothingness
may have broken the food-chain of many insectivores,
especially birds and bats, which are in turn bound to share
that unwelcome distinction of becoming scarce, facing extinction.

David W Daymond

SPOILT, NOT WITH MONEY BUT GREED

Is the air that we breathe really air?
Do we breathe our world because no-one has the courage
                                          to stand up and care?
Are we breathing nature's habitats, trees?
Because that's what it looks like to me!

This surely is not right.
And soon we will have to fight.
Fight to live because the air is gone.
Not breathing air is defiantly wrong.

We have breathed a hole in the ozone layer.
We have breathed oil into the sea.
We have invented Asthma.
So people can suffer like me.

We have climbed every mountain.
We have built on most of the land.
We have started on the rain forest.
Never lent a hand.

We have breathed fumes into the atmosphere.
We have tarmaced all the soil.
We have nearly killed the animals.
Were we given this world to spoil?

Spoilt. Not with money but greed.

Karen Waite (14)

STOP

This planet of ours, was a beautiful place,
It's being destroyed by the human race,
Year by year, a little more,
Humans are changing things galore,
The ozone layer has been caused by gas,
Because it was released in mass,
The temperature seems to be rising,
So the hole in the ozone isn't surprising,
Cutting down the rain forest amist,
The forest would eat a lot of the acids
That were lurking in the atmosphere,
Now drying up, it's everyone's fear,
The power stations do it in haste,
The burning of oil, it is the waste,
Oil refineries burn off the oil,
Smoke up in the skies, takes its toll,
The dumping of waste, into the sea,
Another way to destroy, there has to be,
Toxic waste, in the water flows,
Killing all the seal life, all that shows,
The seals and whales, are getting few,
Man is killing them, for money too,
They call it progress, I call it cruel,
Can't there be a government rule?
And the car is no help to us,
It leaves a smog, the human it does,
A lot of damage, done by man,
Trying to put it right, if they can,
Get rid of the waste, find another way,
Get rid of pollution, a safe world to stay.

Lynn Hallifax

WE WHO SEE

Oh if life was lived in simple vein,
Progress was not such
That people think they need so much
to make them happy -
When so many simple things they could
Achieve themselves
Means happiness they gain.
We use our cars in profusion
When we could enjoy a walk -
But to walk along a road
With large vehicles carrying loads
Traffic in profusion
Does not give you pleasure but fumes
Our air is not fresh many things can corrode.
Nature always triumphs when man for
greed does not destroy.
Is appreciated by all people with eyes to see
They get oh so much joy.
If we feel value for our earth
In this present day.
Give us people with power to turn
Tide to preserving all good
To conserving natural resources
From destruction for gain, stay away.

Victoria Joan Theedam

FOR TOMORROW'S CHILD

Nature created the forest green.
Man made a yellow desert scene.
God created his beautiful garden
and went and called it Eden.
Man from his labours worth
makes machines to destroy this earth.
The rich and dark soil
from his hard toil
grew, blossomed and flourished.
Now the soil with the wind has gone
and man in the sand stands alone.
The tree that gave him shade
from the burning heat of the sun
with one cut he downed what God made.
From the metal he makes his gun
and kills from greed and fun
not necessity and hunger.
When all the beautiful coloured birds have gone
and all the animals dead
what will man eat
as there's no nourishment in cold lead?
Can we stop the cruel destruction now
and save some for tomorrow's child?
Are we ashamed with heads we bow
and wonder what a future, if any,
we have destroyed for many
to justify the greed of a few.

R Medland

SAVE OUR SEAS

Sickening scenes
Of oil and sludge.
Beaches ruined.
It just won't budge.
Sea birds choke
And die in vain.
Seals are hardly seen again.
Volunteers rush
To help the shores,
But tankers pour in
More and more.
Destroy our earth
Why don't you dammit!
After all,
It's only *our* planet.

Moira Brabender

THOUGHTS FOR OTHERS

The way I see things, at this time,
Sad and unable, to justify,
How others can be feeling,
What or who, is the meaning,
Of what's happening to their lives,
Another born, three more die,
I watch and feel the pain,
As it happens, again and again,
For we have everything that we need,
But they cannot feed,
Upon the riches, we ignore,
Which stay forgotten, so too do the poor,
Give up your selfish thoughts, for a while,
Give them the support, make them smile.

Sharon Harwood

MAN'S DREAM

Man's dream,
Was to build a home,
To be secure,
But not alone,
Man's dream
Was to build a town,
Where everyone could live,
Safe and sound.
Man's dream
Was to own all nature,
To kill for money,
To forget hard labour.
Man's dream,
Was to build machines,
To set up factories,
And form a team
Man's dream,
Made God cry,
Smog-filled air,
Dark grey skies.
Animals hurt,
People killed,
Nature forgotten,
Oil spilled.
Oceans almost empty,
Hopes are blown away,
People faced with new problems,
Every single day.
And what about our times,
When love is very rare,
What once was man's greatest dream,
is now everybody's nightmare.

Kerrie Vickers

IS THERE ANYBODY OUT THERE, PLEASE?

London City, where most homeless reside, believe me we do have our pride.
I swallowed down the tight lump in my throat and sunk down under the
damp old coat.
An ache in my heart 'Oh why was I here?' It wasn't meant to happen
like this how did I end up in this fearful abyss?
No-one knows what will happen to the, in this unpredictable world
or when or where they will be hurled.
You could be thrown into deep despair, so beware, there is no guarantee,
we are not free.
People would not now recognise me for now I am a non-entity.
I lost everything, but am too tired to explain to deaf ears who have
not experienced pain.
Government shut their eyes and are quick to condemn
People who walk by say 'Oh look at them!' cold as ice, sleeping in the
gutter with the mice.
Hands red and swollen, feet feel numb, chronic hunger plains in our tum
Filthy, dirty, we're just scum, that's how we are made to feel,
I must now sleep and dream of nice things like a joyous Christmas meal.
Roast Turkey, stuffing and a goblet of sherry, 'Drink and be merry, merry . . .
As heavy tears roll down my cheeks, I cry myself to sleep,
A lonely policeman is looking down on his nightly beat
He does have a look of concern as if he understands, a look of pity
in London City,
He rubs his hands on this dark and dreary night as he walks up along
the street
And as he disappears into the distance so do too the echoes of his feet.
'Thank goodness,' he sighs, as he looks back at where the homeless lie.
Back home to his warm house, with a happy welcome from his spouse.
Spare a little thought for us homeless, I pray, who knows, it might
give strength for another day.

Cathy Lamb

111

MALTA

Expectant.
With your row upon row
Of empty apartment blocks
Waiting for the tourists
To festoon themselves on rocks
Whilst your sea of blue
Touched with a slate green hue
Spreads like velvet round the island.

Along St Paul's bay
The turrets look out
Like citadels on an African coast
And the fishermen sail away
On boats from Phoenician times
Waving cheerfully and looking back
To their Maltese women all draped in black

On an island of Christian fortitude
There rests an air of solitude
And a calm before the storm.

Steve O'Hara

A GENERATION BATHED IN PAIN

Are we a generation bathed in pain
With unexpected hurricanes
In calm backwaters, burnt by acid rain
And an earthquake for the millennium
Could force LA into the sea
A sea of retribution
Abrim with floating carcass
And second hand pollution

Should our desperation be so plain
With unexplained destruction
Will our offsprings' protest be in vain
Whilst a holocaust for the millennium
Keeps us testing weapons for resale
A sale of some confusion
Straight from nuclear textbooks
To darken our own future.

Ade Lullo

MOTHER EARTH

Yielding fruits in season,
Beauty giving reason
And all the means to live,
Your all you freely give.
We your children mostly take
Your bounty, and mistake
Your capacity to regenerate,
So we abuse and infiltrate.
Your balance we destroy,
Claiming minerals and alloy,
We pillage and rape,
Damaging your protective cape
Of ozone, we endlessly fracture,
Harming ourselves by pollution,
Damaging your fruition.
The trees, your lungs, we rob,
Children then struggle with might and main
For vital, life-giving breath,
Many of them slowly choked to death.

E J Whelan

WHAT HAVE THEY DONE TO YOUR BEAUTIFUL EARTH, LORD?

What have they done to your beautiful earth, Lord?
What have they done to your earth?
Thousands of beautiful babies aborted, never allowed to have birth.
Aerosol cans wreaking havoc in the sky.
Radiation sickness making many folk die.
Additives to food causing allergic rash
By non-caring firms just after our cash.
Meat of diseased cows fed to fit cattle
And innocent lambs. Life's a hazardous battle.
Traffic pollution gets worse every day,
Cannot something be invented to disperse it away?
The forests are dying through acid rain.
Man-made pollution the cause, again.
The rainforests, so needed, are being destroyed.
Any laws to restrict this seem null and void.
Some germs and pests are beginning to thrive -
Drugs and poisons to kill them now keep some alive.
They look for new drugs to cure all the ills.
They would do much better to use herbal pills.
Life's a mad rush, to keep up with the best
Which is sometimes the worst. They don't see, in their zest.
Mountains of wasted food, rotting and lying,
While masses of people are starving and dying.
Bombs, knives, and bullets the mortuaries fill.
Animals tortured, in laboratory tests, still,
And, some of your followers, they torture and kill.

Lord, you made the balance just quite right
When you created day and night
And all the living creatures, too,
But, what have they done to us and *you*?

W R Pettitt

IT'S NOT OUR PROBLEM?

Crimes against the planet,
Damage we have done.
The question is, where to start?
The only sure thing being that the end will come.

The ozone layer has a hole,
Rainforests are being cut down.
The Earth is just one big dump,
As country turns to town.

Yet despite all this trouble,
We have the nerve to say . . .
'It's not our problem, why should we care,
we won't be here to pay.'

With that I cannot argue,
It's true that we'll be long gone.
But what about our children's children,
They'll be left to suffer our wrong!

This isn't about not using aerosols,
Or putting rubbish in a bin.
It's all about pride, showing that we can survive,
Providing home and life for our next of kin.

Do you think that we mean anything,
To other planets far away,
They won't care when we've gone, we haven't even been here that long,
So let's show them that we're here to stay!

At least I intend to be anyway!!

Sarah Marley

WHAT HAPPENS NEXT

Man goes about his business
Without a thought for living things
Systematically destroying the rainforests
Polluting all the seas

Contaminating the atmosphere
Until it's no longer any use to breathe
Killing off other species
Not leaving enough to breed

Nature's adapted for millions of years
Cultures so elite to us
Man can undo nature's work in years
Man doesn't care what he does

Man is a blundering biped
Who selfishly thinks of himself
An unwelcome neighbour to life on earth
Who kills his own species as well

He's an unfit keeper of the world
Who'll destroy it if he can
When he's wiped out all the creatures on earth
Maybe man will live with man

Fred Tighe

I SAW

I looked, but never saw,
I touched, but never felt,
All I saw was war,
And all the blood, that's spilt.

The waste, before my eyes,
Of so many young men's lives.
Can we ever count the cost,
Of all the sons we've lost.

Today I looked and saw,
That we must now, stop this war.
Forever onwards it has led,
And never stops, till we are dead.

Today, a young man asked of me,
"Why do you wish, to see me dead.
What have I done, for I don't see.'
'Dear friend, forgive me,' I said.

S Shaw

THE BEACH

Conflicting shoreline tide submitting,
miscellaneous journeyed, matter.

Pebbles in solidarity and length, contain
porous abstract driftwood.

Seaweed colourless drained of life
resemblance to lace.

Shells of varying designs compete with pebbles
in magnitude.

Crisp crackling of shingle occurs underfoot
wet sand and contrasting texture.

Ribbed surface littered with ragworm conspicuous
spiralling signs
sand providing path between receding tide,
scenic coldness arising clouds - pending.

Oil regurgitated by sea-going engines, floats
in an eddy and surrounding channels.

Sand blotched with oil deposits
lamenting beach-comber retires, homeward.

Alan Jones

IN THE NAME OF PROGRESS

Vast rolling hills that range across the land
Are topped by rugged rocks and tall green trees,
Huge plains and meadows reach to sloping sands
Where foamy waves form in the gentle breeze.
The sea surges a raging blue that wields
With wrath waves that crash upon the shore,
A diverse range of life this water shields,
In balance, according to nature's lore,
Above, huge clouds are blown by winds on high,
Great white airships that are always unmanned.
As gracefully they sail across the sky
Their enormous shadows pattern the land,
This great beauty within our atmosphere
Once covered each corner of the earth's sphere.

Cruel concrete now smothers the buried ground
And covers fields in mankind's own chaos,
Fumes choke all life and manic machines sound,
Proclaiming loud that nature's rule is lost.
Superfluous pollution always spills
Into even the deepest of our seas.
This is one of the eco-system's ills,
Man's wretched waste brings Neptune to his knees,
Now sulphuric fumes stain the pale blue sky
And burn away at our ozone layer.
Chemicals will cause lands to become dry,
Mankind's on course to be his own slayer.
It's too late to turn back this ticking clock
But its rotating hands we have to stop.

Chris Scriven

TINDER BOX

Under a relentless sun,
Hills once plush with vegetation,
Standing out boldly in an oasis of green velvets,
Now scorched and parched dusty shades of brown,
Trees shedding their leaves before time,
Beneath their mighty bows the earth cracked and crazed,
Crops burnt to a crisp,
Holes in the ozone layer offering no protection,
The threat of fire hanging over forests and moorland,
Whole regions waiting for the spark to ignite them,
Swallows drop from the clear blue sky like stones,
Then as if not wanting to complete their kamikaze mission
Turn in mid-air with shrill cries and fly off in other directions,
Insects swarm in search of prey,
No succulent vegetation for the greenfly,
Causing ladybirds to swarm and die,
Swarms driving distressed humans from the beaches,
Lie roasted in their billions in the red hot sand,
Shining scarlet shells with their contrasting black spots,
Squawking gulls announce a storm,
Over before it's begun the smell of wet earth,
Now a distant memory as it evaporates in the heat,
Children crying, parents' tempers frayed,
no longer able to rationalise,
All this the heart of an instant no beginning, no end,
Is this the start of man's self destruction,
Or will the elements have the final say,
New roads offer solution from constant pollution,
Others look upon it as a cause for revolution,
The world a tinder box of discontent.

D L Redman

KISS THE EARTH

Kiss the earth and sigh
Then tell this brave new world goodbye
Unless we can change everything we do
Unless we can make heaven on earth come true

Trees cry out and mourn for the lost
While mankind mourns only the cost
It's a crying shame for both of them
When this planet is stripped of all her gems

Ghosts of creatures roam the land
Where beauty stood now concrete stands
And guns speak louder than the birds sing
Because mankind fights over everything

The oceans once were clean and pure
But we have left our mark for sure
The skies that were our new tomorrow
Cry down on us with tears of sorrow

But the free earth will live again
When all of us are long past pain
For nature's power will repossess
And the delicate balance will be redressed

When the earth is free of mankind's curse
When our fate has become the worst
The earth will rise up and be strong
For mankind's history won't last long.

Jenny Smedley

WHAT RIGHT?

What has man done with the trees and the seas?
What gave him the right, to meddle with these?

The trees must be felled; there are houses to build,
The fields will be roads. To the motor we yield.
The sea must be robbed till it holds no more fish,
While factories belch fumes. Much more than we'd wish.

Flower beds must go, to make way for car parks;
The sky must be poisoned to kill the sky larks.
Rainforests must fall, to comply with man's whim,
Tusks ripped from elephant, lion torn limb from limb.

Atomic wastes shall all be dumped in the sea,
And beaches and birds, forbidden to thee.
What has man done, with this unique world of ours?
With his sense, with his brain, and his reasoning powers?

Detergents and effluent can be pumped into rivers,
Rock-face and plateaux should be split into slivers.
Species die out. All blame to the man.
And man must change now, and do what he can.

He has waited too long, to redress the balance,
Now his brain and his sense - are worthless talents.
Man - in his wisdom, has carried on sinning.
The world we have now - was not - time beginning.

What gave man the right to meddle with these?
See - what he's done to the seas and the trees!

Joyce Dobson

PROGRESS OF DEATH

Where once a mighty oak did stand,
A company man brought up the land.
No need for trees or bushes here,
A shopping mall; if these we clear.

Bulldozers thunder, such a din;
People complaining, they cannot win.
Another tree crashes to the ground,
Surely, even prosperity has got its bounds.

But money talks as is the way,
Protesters on deaf ears, do lay.
They tell us it will be okay,
Yet carbon poison, spreads more each day.

Back at their offices, up in the sky,
If they look out the windows,
They should work out why.

For the grime and the dust,
That they clearly see,
Is called smog, and it's caused
By the loss of the tree.

Kenneth Saunders

HELL'S BELLS

Dear A Graham Bell; I write to tell
that your bright idea is now pretty well,
thanks to modern 'advances?' just short of hell!
Now, buzzers and bleeps and gadgets we sell
automated, computerised - oh bring back the bell!
Communication's a riot! Sky - Inter . . . tel . . .
I'd like to dump the lot in a well!

Jane Uff

122

LONG LIVE MOTHER EARTH

What sorrow fills our eyes
As our poor earth just dies
The pain we cause all animals
While we just watch them die

The forest we chop down
The air we will pollute
All animals are caged up
While we steal their food

People are still fighting
And things are getting worse
Our ice-caps are melting
We can't put in reverse

Just stand there and listen
You won't hear a sound
The birds have stop singing
As the word gets around

People are just dying
They are dropping like flies
And all we can do now
Is wait for our time

No more will the whales sing
Or birds fly through the air
As darkness just stays here
And our light as disappeared

Will we ever have learnt
To live life on this earth
To worship all the things
Which needs our mother earth.

Susan Davies

HOW COULD YOU KNOW?

To be amid the crops and trees
You could be forgiven for not knowing that
Anything was wrong with the world.

How could you know that man's avarice
Spreads deadly tentacles,
devouring the very source of life
From the 'unchosen few'
For 'the chosen few' . . .

You could be forgiven for not knowing
That third-world famines are *manmade* . . .
Those haunting silhouettes of meagre life
Depicting 'man's inhumanity to man'.

You could also be forgiven for not knowing
That strong countries take from
weak countries;
Raping their natural resources
Even though these simply mean survival -
and nothing else - for the 'unchosen few'.

And you could be forgiven for not know that
The laws of 'eco' dynamics dictates:
'Resource-intensive over production'
Leads to over-intensive human consumption . . .
For the 'chosen few' . . .

In the scheme of things
The 'unchosen few' do not seem important:
they are not competitive;
not consumers: *so*
'Feel free' walk into their larders.
Take what they have. 'Have a nice day!'
Civilise the natives - wherever.
Try to make them live like you.
Ensure that they make money
To buy from you
What *they* already had.

Hannah Yates

GOD'S CREATION

What is happening to this dear old world?
The power and greed of man
Causing pollution and animals to be culled
Money and profit taking first place
Debasing the whole of the human race
A quick 'buck' for the present
No thought for the future - come what may
Our children growing up and having no say
The beauty of nature and fauna being destroyed
Leaving less, to the future generation, to be enjoyed!
What has happened to man's humanity to man?
As time goes by he's an 'also ran'
Machines taking over men's skills
Leaving fewer jobs for people to fill
Terrorism, violence and laxity in morals
Endangering the world with so many foibles.
The whole human race will have to think again
Doing their best to amend or - this beautiful world
Will come to an end!!

Janet Wallace Wight

OUR WORLD

How thankful we should be
That God gave us eyes to see.
The beauty all around us on earth, and up above.
The different seasons' flowers, the trees,
With autumn changing all their leaves
Then winter comes and paints things white
And frost glistens with a silvery light.

Look up above, you may see a sky of blue
With clouds drifting by, like puffs of cotton wool,
At night-time when the sky is dark
The moon is there to light it up
Millions of stars blinking at you, as you look up.

And what about the beautiful birds around
The cuckoo, the singing lark
The aviaries of lovely birds in the parks
We take for granted the beauties of the world
That God put here for man to realise their worth.

Winifred Ordidge

NOTHING FOR THE CHILDREN

When all the earth is desert, and all the trees are dead,
When no birds sing up in the sky, no flowers raise their heads,
When humming bees flit in and out of artificial bowers,
Who will tell the busy bees,
There's no pollen in the flowers,
Who will tell the children there's nothing left for them,
We've killed the earth, we've killed the sea,
We've killed it all - *amen!!*

L Chidlow

126

OUR PLANET

When first there was the atom bomb
That was a hell of thinking for everyone
If it would, be ever used?
And who would be the first to be accused
It did go off in Hiroshima
The devastation caused a lot of hysteria
People from the world tried to get it banned
Before it destroyed our lovely land
What were these men thinking when this bomb was made
To destroy our land in one decade
There was no need for this deterrent
Man could put his brains to better elements
We have to look after and love our earth
And not destroy life, for what it's worth
And think much more on the theme to love
And not destroys our heaven's above.

Jean Linney

THE OAK TREE

The old oak tree has stood three hundred years.
Its leaves are fluttering with new-fangled fears.
Nothing has filled it with such dreadful fright.
As this new by-pass swinging from the right.

The developers have flexed commercial muscle.
They don't care for the old tree's frightened rustle.
Protesters tried to protect it all in vain.
The bulldozers are worse than acid rain.

The protesters have now all been swept away.
Here comes the saws, the tree begins to sway.
Goodbye old tree, and all three hundred years.
It took this lot to justify your fears.

Denys Kendall

127

POISONED EARTH

Our time on this planet is on a very short lease,
but don't you fret, for we may yet,
be saved by Greenpeace.
For 25 years they have pleaded with the governments
that be
to stop the pouring of pollutants into our seas.

They warn that the air we breathe is filled with smog and fumes,
that slowly our children's lives it does consume,
while overhead the hole in the ozone does loom,
bringing forth ultimate doom.

Gone are our forests, tropical and green,
now it's as if they never had been.
Why is it? That we treat Mother Nature so mean.

Is this the beginning of the end?
So it does seem!

Phillip N Dawson

MIST FROM THE MOUNTAINS

If this morning's mist should never lift
    From these fair hills,
We'd never know their green again
    Or springtime's frills -
Then all these scenes I love so well
    Forever lost!
No sun to warm the land around
    At untold cost;
Forever grey, endless grey
    And always damp,
A twilight world, excluding light
    Dims the lamp.

Wendy P Frost

THE HOUR

The hour is here (or may be past), when our vast and lovely tether
Has shown the time has come, at last, to act or die together . . .

As snow falls o'er the tropics a thaw is melting the poles,
And a wide blue sky (where missiles fly), is punctured full of holes.
Now we drink poison oxides in water from toxins discharged in the soil,
Sea-birds and once golden beaches are stricken and blighted by oil,
We are digesting chemicals daily, lead, as we breathe in the air,
Acidic rain is falling again killing rivers and lakes everywhere.
While the time bomb of nuclear waste (from our roaring power stations),
Are quietly ticking away for future generations,
Who, if they bathe in our waters or paddle and play in the sea,
Must swim against sewage and faeces . . . is this our legacy?
For with every slick and spillage . . . every annihilation,
With every infant inhaler or guideline violation . . .
We are reaping our own deadly harvest from the careless seeds we
                                                          have sown . . .
A crop of filth and destruction that with our children have grown.
Pollution is running amok . . . still we are killing the whale,
Starvation and warfare have soared to such a terrible scale
That I fear we have now reached the point when the dreadful outcome
                                                          could be
Not a curse . . . but a God granted blessing . . . ending this misery . . .

The hour is slipping (it may be gone), when this vast and lovely tether
Has shown the time, at last, has come to act or die . . . together.

Anthony Hilton

THE CHASE PLAINS

Take me by the horns, dear boy,
take me by the horns,
'til my eyes bleed thorns, old boy,
take me by the horns.

Sound the horns now, dear boy,
sound those blesséd horns,
rape all that adorns, dear boy,
come sound those sacréd horns.

Follow me over here, old chum,
follow me over here,
these fields are very clear, old chum,
so follow me over here.

Chase me to my death, dear man,
follow and chase my death,
chase my last breath, dear man,
come see the plains of death.

The pleasure is all mine, good friend,
the pleasure is all mine,
drink my blood like wine, good friend,
come drink and swallow my prime.

Andy McPheat

THE EARTH IS A FURNACE

As the generations grow it becomes apparent,
The Earth is getting hotter.
The icebergs are melting, the rivers are rising,
Is there anything we can do?

As global gases are emitted,
The environment must suffer and burn.
A hole through our lives,
That gets bigger each spray.

130

A great furnace fuelled by ignorance,
A burning heart that no-one can douse.
A tree comes to the rescue,
And gets beaten to a pulp.

Life might adjust, or it might die,
What is essential is change.
The Earth is crying out for help,
But no-one will listen or attend.

Dawn Louise Bell

LIFE'S NADIR

As we the far horizons pause to view
O'er the sea of romance and mystery,
'White horses' gaily toss their foaming manes
And sea birds over many oceans flew

The land birds charm our ears with sweetest tone
And countless creatures roam our textured land;
Lush green fields know the cycle of God's peace,
And oceans deep hold rule amongst its own.

Those words alas, will only memories be
Should foolish man God's gift of life renounce,
Starvation, and world death will surely come
Through an insatiable insanity.

And yet, man's obsession for wealth and power
Rejects the wonders of our fragile earth,
Polluted land and sky and sea, and man
With uncaring greed swells his ivory tower.

Will God's supreme patience finally lapse
And with a second 'flood' our lives despatch;
With woeful regret God may cleanse His earth
From human-kind, and start again perhaps.

Geoff Hague

MY BEACH

When I was little, I sat on the sand,
I dug with my spade, I dug with my hand.
I made a sand castle, it seemed big to me.
Because I was small, it came up to my knee.

I sat in my pushchair and looked at the sea.
The sun on the water was glinting at me,
The waves rippled gently on to the beach,
Bringing up seaweed and shells to my reach.

People around me were happy and gay,
They came to the beach to spend all the day.
Lots of ice creams got gobbled down,
Children were happy, never a frown.

This year I went back to play on that sand.
To dig with my spade, and to dig with my hand,
To make a sand castle, as big as could be,
With a moat going round it, to reach to the sea.

But as I got near it, what did I see?
Nothing but rubbish as far as could be.
Crisp bags and bottles, chip trays and tins,
Things that the people should put in the bins.

The sea didn't sparkle, or gleam back at me,
It was dirty and grey and as dull as could be.
Rubbish was floating where I wanted to swim,
And sewage was floating right up to the rim.

People beside me wore large orange macks,
They worked for the council and carried large sacks,
To pick up the rubbish that was left on the sand,
In case they got cut they had gloves on their hands.

I wish I could go back and play on clear sand,
To dig with my spade and to dig with my hands.
To splash in clean water and swim in clean sea.
These things would make me as glad as can be.

Susan Briggs (9)

SOMEONE IS DESTROYING THE EARTH

Someone is destroying millions of trees,
Dumping harmful chemicals into the seas,
Spreading toxic-waste across the land,
Making the world uninhabitable for man,
They are pumping carbon-monoxide into the air
And that certain someone doesn't seem to care,
They're not worried about the years ahead,
When the damage is done they'll be dead,
Are they so ignorant? That they don't know,
That from toxic-waste cancers will grow,
That when waves lap against the shore,
It will leave the marine life that is no more,
That when carbon-monoxide rises into the air,
It slowly burns a hole through the ozone layer,
Every year the cases of asthma have increased,
Some of the livestock we eat has become diseased,
Ultra-violet rays are blistering delicate skins,
Tides are rising as the ice-bergs are melting,
The world is changing because someone is changing it,
By playing with nature's balance and re-arranging it,
Someone doesn't realise how much their life is worth,
Without a thought someone is destroying the earth.

Kathleen Speed

THE UNIVERSE IS NOT MY OWN

The universe is not my own
   And neither yours to rule
Indifference I do not condone
   But compromise I do
We never learn by our mistakes
   So obviously we
Are bound those same blunders to make
   for all eternity.

Granted you cannot be blamed
   for wrongs done by your kin,
Though you (you claim) are truly shamed
   By all your father's sin
Violets be us everyone
   When accusations fly
In unison we swiftly run
   To shelter and deny.

Self-motivated and self-crowned
   The kings and queens of all
And those that fail to tread be drowned
   As those that rise shall fall.
I dare not say I'm blinded
   Or complain it isn't bright
When daily I'm reminded
   That 'twas I turned out the light.

Year in and out and without hitch
   This world we do abuse
Not only have we flicked the switch
   We've taken out the fuse.

Debbie Charles

PARADOX TO THE FUTURE

Flashes of light shot across the midnight sky
Eyes looking upwards wondering why
The earth would never be the same
Since the past had erupted and this future came
Police patrolled the steaming streets

Guns at the ready for the next scavenging freak
Hundreds hurried on to their destined place
Big brother watched and marked the number on their face
Children played at home as the robot carried out its daily tasks
Mothers and fathers lost expression no need to ask

Why the clinical room did not look quite like home any more
This was the outcome after the ultimate World War
The old lady shuffled by glad to get home
Rags for clothes little food back to where she lived alone
The churches were quiet lost to the world
But yes I see a very small girl
Eyes looking upwards to the figure of Christ
Pleading for a time when maybe there might
Be hope for them all
As the acid rain outside quietly begins to fall
Suddenly a light streamed over the praying child
Promising a second coming of Christ beyond the world of the while
Mankind must heed the warnings of any more wars
Give the children hope for their dreams to store

Julia Haywood

DEVASTATING EARTH

Planet decaying
Earth we are slaying
Destroying the world around
Atmosphere poor
When the ozone's no more
Darkness will be found
Forests in ruin
What are we doing
I really think we don't know
Our future obscure
Feeling unsure
And what have we to show
Violence and war
Why? What for?
For what is there to fight
We'll go on this way
Lead the planet astray
And so put out the light.

Jacqueline Griffiths

VIOLATION OF MOTHER NATURE

A beauty, quite beyond belief,
Raped by unrelenting thief.
Decay of wilderness and reef
Bear testimony to her grief.

Stuffing; dumping; spewing; crushing.
Screaming out? Just keep on pushing!
Endless spurts of filth sent gushing
To challenge her impotent flushing.

Our indulgence, year on year
Washed by sweet, acidic tear.
She calls, but no-one waits to hear;
Gripped by Envy, Greed and Fear.

We spurn her hurt, imploring glance.
Dismissive; fat with arrogance.
She stumbles: Spent: No more to dance
And knows - there'll be *no second chance.*

Pamela Daniels

BLACK DEATH

Oh mighty tanker, sailing our coastal sea
Spewing your lethal cargo causing catastrophe,
Your massive tanks contain black death, as you sail the oceans wide,
Where your sister ships have run aground, all wild life has died,
You hug the coast then run aground, and there you break your back,
Your ruptured tanks discharges death in sludge of brown and black

Your vile slick that's miles wide just snakes across the sea
To bring to dolphins, seals and birds death and misery,
Now you're at rest upon the rocks, and your load of death is lost
All those who say they're not to blame must begin to count the cost,
Cormorants, guillemots, gulls and puffins too
Will die in their thousands off our coast, and all because of you

The aftermath will last for months, your spill has done its worst,
Your leaking tanks and waves of crude is a disgusting curse,
And now the worst has happened, and your slick spreads far and wide
Who will say I'm sorry when a thousand birds have died,
Who will say it's my fault, who will take the blame,
As long as there are mighty tankers we shall see the same again.

Finlay Shiner

SEWAGE FARMING

When earth was new and free from all defilement;
When God had brought about His wildest dream;
Before man brought about his own revilement
The whole damned world was fresh and Harpic-clean.

When Gaia danced and sang in all her glory,
And no-one smelt the stench of fetid air;
In the days of this late-lamented fairy story,
All men breathed free, and rats kept to their lair . . .

Now the world's a chamber pot, a near-filled midden,
A dying planet fated to decay;
For wisdom knew the truth - to fools it's hidden -
That entropy will have the final say . . .

Thus ordure rules, along with scum and litter,
Cracked sewage pipes emit their endless muck
And the need for harmful bleach makes many bitter -
While they moan about the cost of Toilet Duck!

While we walk on Slime-Bag Street in Garbage City,
Regretting what our children must accept -
The whited-walls who spew forth in committee
Accuse the hoi polloi of gross neglect.

Now sediment of humankind roams wild,
And we need to fumigate each fly-blown mind;
Unearth the Eden from which we were exiled,
To flush the toilet we have left behind.

Though entropy's, in fact, God's in-built ending -
And everything is destined to decay . . .
With a little bit of Harpic and pipe-mending
Then perhaps tomorrow may not come today.

J Margaret Service

DYING RACE

Can you feel the dog as it lifts its leg against your trunk?
Can you really breathe in the smog and fog and gunk?
Do you wish that you could move and make your getaway?
To somewhere where the air is clean and the sky is not grey.
Can you hear your friends scream as they tumble to the ground?
Do you wish you could cover your ears and block out the sound?
Do you remember when there was green grass here,
when the air was pure and the water was so clear?
Did your ancestors tell you stories about the time before,
Before humans destroyed them and brought about this downfall?
Can you fell your bark slowly crumbling and peeling?
Do you know that the fumes are stopping your wounds healing?
Can you feel the dry, new wind that blows through your fingers.
As it brings the fallout which smothers as it lingers?
Did you feel the Earth rumble as World War 3 began,
Did your roots then tremble with the foolishness of man?
Will you tell your seedlings - if you live to tell this tale,
Would you still remember when the horizon went so pale?
Can you see what's left of all your neighbouring oaks?
Or have you been affected by the dust that blinds and chokes?
Can you see that all the other trees around have gone?
Do you feel your wizened roots that were once so very strong?
Do you think that you - an ancient, leaning wise oak tree,
Could forgive the human race for its endless folly?
Will you remember all that happened when man's plan went wrong,
Did you tell your children that the end will not be long?
Now that you have fallen to the ground with one last cry . . .
Your seedlings spread your wisdom,
        for the knowledge must not die.

Melissa Kelly

LOVE IS ASK OF THEE . . . OH BARREN LAND . . .

Here in our village
We have no food. I'd eat sand
If I though it would do any good
There's a war inside my tummy
Belly swollen . . . as my stomach
Quietly consumes itself . . .

Love I ask of thee oh barren land . . .

Here in our fields . . . we have no crop
There has been no rain now for a long time
And water to my lips . . . would be like wine . . .
Children are dying here every day
Because of disease that won't go away
White man come . . . take a good look
To him we are a 'story book . . . '

They promise us help but it never come
White man won't get off his bum
We have waited long
In the heat of the sun . . .

Love I ask of thee oh barren land . . .

For there was a war that was never won
With starvation and sickness
To overcome
And you in brick houses are the lucky ones
Love I ask of thee oh barren land . . .

Isn't there anyone . . . to give a hand . . .

Sally Wyatt

ACID TEARS

The wild dragon, drew a dragon's breath,
As angels danced on distant thunder clouds,
As nature winces at her own untimely death,
Mankind screams in defiance, at her ever darkening shroud.

Greedy little businessmen, with sweaty little hands,
Short term profit, an ambitious dream,
Ignorant uncaring about vast polluted wastelands,
Poor tortured planet, one can almost hear her scream.

Earth now weeps only acid tears,
And breathes lung lining caustic air,
Yet still the traffic fumes confirm our fears,
As the tortured innocent lie, in the forests of despair.

As a variety of species of beautiful life, now daily die,
And trees that once provided healthy air, are hewn,
As millions throughout the world, in hunger cry,
The more fortunate, are fed by silver spoon.

Increasing populations, creating increasing pollution,
More extinction, more hunger, more sorrow,
When wars seem to some, the only solution,
Yet never a thought for the 'morrow.

Good old days, bad new ways, tomorrow never comes,
As warnings ignored, lay abandoned on the seas of hope,
Future expectations, and wistful dreams succumb,
The truth is, the planet simply cannot cope.

Jeremy Charles William Bloomfield

DESTRUCTION BY MAN

Man is a total destroyer
just look at what he's done
There is only one earth in the universe
and now it's all but gone.
Nature is a balance of wonder
a law unto itself
but man came along and took over
and tipped one side of the shelf.
So many things will never return
our children will now never see
but there will always be buildings
and wars and crimes
and it's thanks to you and me.

Dorothy Johnstone

NUCLEAR POWER TO THE LAND

All nuclear plants are next to the sea,
and often in areas of outstanding visibility.
These areas are large, and full of wildlife zest,
so the power plants' role is to protect and make the best.

Now this landscape, designated as the new heritage coast,
is in areas of outstanding natural beauty, they boast.
'We are actively involved in planting broad leaf trees,'
to encourage that proliferation of the birds and bees.

There are willow warblers, tits and blackcaps and all else,
nature trails, open classrooms, out at the nature's pulse.
There will be bird hides, and those field study centres.
Now with those panoramic views, it only attracts caravans and tenters.

Alan Noble

DESTINY?

What is the world coming to?
Where will it all end?
Where is the world going to?
If wars we can't mend?

Evil aggression, terrorists' acts,
hatred and violence,
uprisings and pacts.
Sorrow and suffering
for the young and the old,
No freedom and liberty,
actions daring and bold.
Little children at risk,
hard drugs being sold,
Lock up the villains,
cowards, cunning and cold.

The world is a battlefield,
where is there peace?
Bombings and murders,
such destruction must cease.
Innocent victims caught up in the fight
Thugs on the rampage causing damage by night.

When men can be brothers, respecting mankind
And leaders with wisdom and dignity find
Strength and compassion and courage to give
People their right, peace, and freedom to live.

Joan Heybourn

STOP BEFORE IT'S TOO LATE

Leave the rainforests as they were meant
God made them so, they were Heaven sent
Beauty is being destroyed today
By those who want to have their own way

There are healing powers within the trees
Medicines made from many leaves
Helping people regain their health
It's more important than having wealth

Beauty is around us everywhere
But man today doesn't seem to care
If only they could see it so
But everything nice just has to go

Leave this world of ours alone
Valley, river, rock and stone
Have it as God meant it to be
Let everyone of us feel free

Ozone layers and global warming
Should be taken as a warning
Can they not see the harm they do
They should remember it's our world too

Molly Andrew

JUDGEMENT ON THE HUMAN APHIDS

If only we could stand back and see
That we are global garden pests,
The ones who kill the beneficial plants.
Perhaps before it is too late the
Gardener will come and spray us all.

Rosa Barbary

NEWCASTLE-ON-SEA
(Crimes against the planet)

Newcastle didn't used to be by the sea, son.
The coast stretched for miles on and on.
Whitley Bay, Tynemouth, South Shields.
Then global warming came and the damage was done.

People along the coast lost their homes,
The Metro railway had to be re-routed,
So many miles of Tyneside under water,
The seas rose high, the world had been polluted.

No where's a pier by the City Hall
That used to be ten miles inland.
The high street shops, McDonalds, Burger King
Are on the beach and surrounded by sand.

The rainforest has been destroyed,
The fossil fuel is all gone.
Now nuclear power is all they use,
What other things could go wrong?

Malcolm Lisle

AWARENESS

How often we mention the harm to our world
Slightly smug that we have recycled a bottle or can.
A gesture indeed - but how minute!
In the minuscule of time that is the twentieth century
Without thought or care we destroyed eons of evolution.
It is too late to save the earth?
The young have more awareness
But will their voice be heard?
The millennium approaches
Should we celebrate or despair?

V Bechaalani

145

EARTH ABUSE

This azure globe, amid dark space,
So much beneath is out of place.
Such beautiful pleasures the earth does hold,
But, the dangers now present are manifold.

The oceans are being filled with waste,
The forests are being burned in haste.
The skies are darkened by clouds of dust,
Many past treasures now turned into rust.

Much blood has been shed in the battles of war,
Explosions have shaken the earth to its core.
Drought and starvation are the fate of many,
Some have so much, some have not any!

Animals are killed for monetary gain,
As onlookers, we are humbled by shame.
We hold them in zoos, their freedom we take,
A few disagree and protest for their sake.

Elephant is hunted for the price of his tusk,
Gorilla is shot by poachers at dusk.
Whale is harpooned for his versatile oil,
Dolphin's intelligence condemns him to toil.

Air is polluted by exhaust fumes from cars,
Landscape bears many, very ugly scars.
Green fields are replaced by concrete and glass,
Life in the nineties has become such a farce!

Chemicals are sprayed all over the land,
Crops are much healthier when untouched by hand!
Rivers may fill with filthy, green sludge,
Those in command, this issue will fudge!

So, what happens next? Can the planet we save?
Do we really care? Are we really brave?
Must we so abuse the world? Condemn it to dust?
So much we must change, in mankind place our trust!

Pat Drew

ONE HUNDRED THOUSAND

One hundred thousand passers by
Just cannot know my anguish
Well kept from view with steely face
From this state in which I languish

One hundred thousand days go by
As I seek to make a difference
A voice within the multitude
So desperate for deliverance

One hundred thousand tears are cried
That reflect the situation
The carriages of injustice
That scream deliberation

One hundred thousand stars on high
Frequent the nightly vastness
I urge them all to intervene
And stop this earthly madness

One hundred thousand dreamers sigh
Who defend our aspirations
My allegiance goes to all of these
Such hope precedes salvation.

David Whitby

CARING FOR CREATION

Birds fly high overhead -
Habitat surveying.
Secretly die beneath -
Nature's world-decaying.

Through ephemeral eyes
Eroding effigies -
Depleted, destroy lands,
Wasting effete bodies.

Earth's perpetual defence -
Arms against pollution.
Fragment rose petal hopes -
Bloom humane solution.

Environment think tank,
Green party people care.
Protect ozone-melt world,
Educate children there.

Just thoughts, forward planning,
Fair future, now - this day -
Preserve life's tomorrow,
Recycle growth, care today.

Hilary Ann Morris

DESTRUCTION

This planet of ours is crying
Plants and trees are dying
Earth is turning into sand
Due to the nature of man

Spectacular trees stood tall and proud
Till man came along and shouted aloud
Cut them down, make more space
Down came the trees, lost was their grace

When will man take heed
He's had enough warnings indeed
This planet is beautiful, rolling hills, blue the sea
Now it's polluted with help from you and me

A haze where the sun should be shining through
The ozone layer thinning, skies no longer blue
Ice caps will start melting, the flooding will begin
To spoil our planet of beauty is the most awful sin

Man is genius
So surely he can see
The damage he is doing
If I can, why can't he?

Pamela Smith

THE EARTH CRIES

Pulsing as a heartbeat the Planet cries, oh inhabitants stop!
When you break my core my life will diminish, leading to oblivion
How dare you assault me and expect me to support your life
My land, my air, and my seas are gifts
You persist on polluting with your progressive ways
Remember, I am the maker and the deliverer
If you love me then cease your destruction of me

Already my rain is filled with acid, my air filled with smog
My land filled with chemicals, oh how bitter the smell
Already you die of cancers never heard before
But still you refuse to accept the warning signs

Begin anew and be sparing with my resources
Be less greedy in your needs and progress by nature's path
Remove your chimneys, seek knowledge to run your ships at sea
Clean your sewage, you already know how, don't cut the costs
Learn by nature's ecosystem to grow healthy crops
Allow my rain to seep beneath the ground and replenish aquifers
Therefore, plant grass and trees where old concrete once lay
Refurbish the old and make into new, in kind with nature.

For all those who help with love and generosity
To correct the danger that has soiled my body
My spirit will remember them should fires rage over me
If all attempts be too late and man's spirit is defeated

To those in authority who hold the reigns, lend your ears
For you may topple first should the ending be inevitable
Because you will not listen to the whaling of my cries
You hear only your own selfish heart and deal in rude compromises
For if my world be delivered into hell for the sake of hell
So too will man be delivered by the molten lava
And will come to know the agony of my defeat

Jacqueline Butler

150

LOOK AFTER OUR PLANET

Have you ever stopped to wonder
The power of mankind
The sort of things he can do
and decisions he can mind
he can push the button of the bomb
to make the mushroom cloud
he can decide our future no matter
if we yell and shout real loud.
Who gives these people the right
to tell us what to do
who gives these people the right
to damage our planet the way they do.
They cut down our rainforests
and kill our life on land
why do they push aside the food
of the helping hand
We could all help to make this world
a happier place to be
if only mankind would stop killing
the flower and the buzzing bee.
These people should really be
put away for good
or taught to live the good life
that good people should
These crimes against our planet
don't help anyone of us
so look after your planet the way you should
and stop creating all this fuss.

Lori

MEMORIES . . . (YEAR: 2075)

My grandmother told me a story today,
About great forests
Where she once used to play,
Trees - sixty feet high!
With branches that pierced a clean blue sky,
She told me of streams - crystal clear,
And of animals -
Foxes, squirrel and deer,
She told me of fields of ripened corn,
And the beauty of every sunset and dawn,
Oceans that lapped golden sands,
Breathtaking snow-topped mountainous land,
Ancient woodland filled with nightingale's song,
Until it all began to go disastrously wrong . . .
There was a tear in her eye
When she sadly spoke,
(Bitterness had devoured her remaining hope),
'My child, our ancestors ignored the warning call,
And through their ignorance, they lost it all . . .'

Tara Jane Scriggins

THE OZONE LAYER

The condensed active oxygen one can get,
Just walking along in the sun.
You do not have to lay on the beach or sit on a chair,
For it can get you anywhere.
So please beware.

One's flesh will be tender;
One can hardly bear to touch.
I'm telling you all, if it gets you;
You will not like it very much.

It is also very active
And it will not get any better.
The larger the hole, the worse it will be,
And maybe we shall very soon see.

I wish man would not interfere
In God's most wonderful and beautiful world.
Then we would not live in so much fear
And most of us would be of good cheer.

Amy Barrett

WHAT ON EARTH IS GOING ON

The end of the world is nigh; is it heck!
There's plenty of life in the old planet yet
Question is, what life will it sustain?
The global chemistry sets, which thoughtless progress feeds
Emit matter, disproportionate to mother nature's needs
A human trait to pass the buck; no-one takes the blame

The end for some species is close; perhaps it is
If nature's union is broken, there's no solace in its kiss
Some fated gene, may herald calls for action
And a gallant crusade, for this worldly cause
But not whilst mankind, savours cruelty and wars
The instinct for power's a major distraction

Mankind will see the light; in the end
Maybe (not) too late, for the world to befriend
In betweentimes plans, are unnatural solutions
Genetic ways and intensive farming
Favour growth, not stability; all that's alarming
Sounding even more vibes, for gloomy conclusions

Graham Miller

WHY?

Why do most people have to destroy, not respect
The things that surround them? Or at best neglect;
And carry along as if they have sole right
To life, never mind living
And ignore the plight
Of animals giving
Their lives for our pleasure, to eat or to wear
Never knowing the sunlight , or wind in their hair
The stars in the sky, or the taste of fresh grass
They stand in a cage, while their few short months pass
And what have they left to look forward to then?
A harrowing journey, then throat slit by men.

It's not just the animals - man ruins the scenery
And builds monstrous structures, where once there was greenery
They sit in their offices, planning more ruin
Their driver is greed - ever more profit
They don't think what they're doing
It's money - must make more of it.
They pollute and contaminate, block out the light.
Of all earthly creatures, just man causes blight.
If all men would try to give more than they take
It might not be too late to erase the mistake
And try to repair damage done over years
So man doesn't need to cry crocodile tears.

Rosalyn Nancarrow

THE ONLY WAY

Our Lord looked down
from the Hill of Calvary,
engulfed in agony -
of the Cross He bore -
The Sins of the World
crucifying His Whole Body.

Without God we're nothing -
there's crimes drugs and wars,
the World's becoming lost
we don't know where we are.
We think that man's knowledge
will bring Peace and Goodwill -
but our greed for possessions
it's purpose will kill.

Earth's troubles are man-made
we self-persecute,
each blame the others -
many blame God.
Yet we know in our hearts
that we're really to blame -
The free-will He gave to us
we've misused in His Name.

'Look at Me' He pleads
looking down from the Cross -
'Ask and Receive -
I'll bring Peace to your hearts.'

Mary Skelton

OUR CHANGING PLANET

This planet of ours is slowly, falling into decline,
With oil polluted beaches and rivers full of slime.
Tall chimneys pouring filthy smoke into the skies above,
That falls to earth as acid rain, on the planet that we all love.
Nuclear waste and toxic waste, plastics by the ton
How do we get rid of them? The job will never be done.
Satellites orbiting out in space, at thousands of miles an hour,
Will fall back to earth one day, causing a meteorite shower.
The tropical forests are being destroyed that is home for many a creature,
A hole has appeared in the ozone layer upsetting the balance of nature.
Sea birds are being washed ashore, fighting to stay alive,
With feathers all covered in thick black oil, let's hope they will survive.
Gangs roam the plains of Africa with rifles at the ready,
Hunting for herds of elephants to kill just for their ivory.
Callous nations with factory ships roam the seven seas,
Searching for schools of friendly whales, to kill with utmost ease.
The food we eat the liquids we drink will never be the same,
They're full of *E's* and additives, I think we should complain.
So let us work together to save our planet from destruction,
And let us all remember, there will be future generations.

Rupert F Lewis

EARTH APPEAL

Planet of water
Veiled in blue
What has man in his short time
Done to you?

Exploded the atom,
Blasted with bombs,
Polluted the rivers,
Air poisoned by fumes.

Littered the seabed
Outerspace too
Holed the ionosphere
Disaster now due!

Is it too late to save you?
Can we say *stop* in time?
Let's stand up to befriend you
Before it's countdown!

Avrille Oxley McCann

MELTDOWN?

Nineteen ninety six and we're in a fix
There's a hole in the sky we cannot repair,
As long as the money, (though it may seem funny)
Keeps filling our pockets do we really care.
We've all heard the warning about global warming
The decline of the poles and the greenhouse effect,
The oceans are rising and is it surprising
That we are the cause through our need and neglect.
We dig and we mine and it all seems just fine
But what will then happen when the resources run dry,
From the oil we pump to the waste that we dump
Is turning the world into a filth-ridden sty.
And the suits in high places with leather briefcases
Sit in the boardroom and look on with mirth,
And we're just to blame for playing the game
Where the only result is the death of our earth.
There are no reserves so we must preserve
This planet of ours for our children to see,
Let's not be idle or remain suicidal
Or the time will come when we cease to be.

Duncan Armour

THE MURDER OF A PLANET

There where once great forests
Where tall trees stood,
They've chopped them all down
To make firewood
The oak and elm
Once stood with grace,
Now they've built factories
to stand in their place.

They've polluted the waters
with oil and grime.
Now instead of clear water
the fish swim through slime,
In the great flowing river
Where the salmon once bred
There's nothing now living,
The fish are all dead.

Buds barely blossom,
Plants no longer grow,
Birds no longer sing,
Flowers wilt in the sun's glow.
Chemical dumping caused
Most creatures to die
The bird with oil soaked feathers
has no chance to fly.

So what can we do
To make amends
To the mindless destruction
of our animal friends,
can we change?
Or is it too late?
Will mankind suffer
a similar fate?

Michael Howe

NUCLEAR NEEDS

What's nuclear next
We've got nuclear physics
Providing nuclear bombs
Then nuclear power
And yet more bombs

The next war'll be nuclear
We've had accidents
Causing contamination
We've had explosions
And more radiation

Nuclear power gives electricity
And radioactive waste
Which is buried and left
We leave it for our children
And their children to clean up

Is it worth it
Those in power say yes
This power is needed
But is it I think not
It's leading to war

Earth provides power
But we don't use it
We make our own
While killing her
What's nuclear next

With more bombs
And senseless politicians
We're heading for war
And guess what's next
Within the hour it's nuclear earth.

Jamie Williams

POLLUTION

If you could cut the air in half,
Inside you would see,
All the way along the path,
It's black and dirty.

There's not a clear patch in sight,
The air is polluted,
But doesn't it give you a great big fright,
To know that's what we did.

And off we go with our cars and sprays,
Polluting everywhere,
But this I know the whole world prays,
Without even a care.

And now the ice from both the poles,
Has melted - every bit,
And all that's left are the barren holes,
Where life used to sit.

Brijal Doshi

THE PATH OF PROTEST

When planners plan a motorway,
Protesters line up for the fray,
    Aghast, abusive, fairly fraught -
    There's a battle to be fought.
Not in *my* back yard, they say,
With Nimbyism holding sway.

When planners plan a motorway,
Protesters always have their say.
    They raise petitions, voices, flags;
    Appear appalled in local rags;
Write letters heavy with dismay:
They don't need a motorway.

But when it's finally decreed,
Appeals dismissed and plans agreed,
>>And when it's built and there to stay,
>>Protesters use it every day,
Proving their mysterious need
Of cant, hypocrisy and speed.

John Slim

THE INVASION

They came one fine spring morning
With their 'monsters' made of steel.
They chopped down the line of poplars,
With such speed it seemed unreal.
Then hedges and trees were razed to the ground,
With sickening thuds and crashes.
With nests full of eggs, they were put in a pile,
And by evening were nothing but ashes.

Then they brought along bricks and concrete,
And put up houses, row upon row,
'Squeeze them all in, as many as can be,
We don't want any grass to grow.
The people who'll live here won't need space,
They don't want gardens or privacy,
Squash in as many homes as we can,
It'll mean all the more money for me.'

They left one cold winter morning,
With no thought for the trees that had died,
They took their noisy, steel monsters,
And another piece of our green countryside.

Susan Wooden

161

TOMORROW MAY COME
(For Trana-Rebecca)

Small minded rapists carve terror through perfect wilderness
With wealth and greed their only
motivation they choke and crush all in their path.
Leaving only death in their wake.
Wild animals are slaughtered confirming
the ignorance and arrogance of man
While a pincer movement is performed
on the earth's core by mindless men
with a wish for destruction.
Earth sea and air are toxin filled,
and in a world where to breathe is
to be contaminated.
There may be no future at all.

Paul Gray

LEIGH MARSH

What do these waving stands of grass
Know of the increased ozone about them,
Or the delicate pink rose
Care about the trash buried beneath its roots?

What concern does the hawk have for the seeping methane
As it hovers above the cowering harvest mouse
Or the ducks for the prismatic fluids
Streaking their tidal ponds?

My dogs trot around the man-made paths
Oblivious to the whining of the model aircraft
As do I on a hot summer's day
When a cool breeze brings with it
The unmistakable scent of rotting cockle-shells.

Brian MacDonald

LIFELESS GREEN

Spores of black on field of green,
between the blades of grass an oily sheen.
Pock marked ruts where rubbish lays,
mars the scene on sunny days.

Branches bent all brown and bare,
lifeless forms just lying there.
Hedges trampled flattened down,
sorry sight this broken crown.

Muddy pools a soggy mess,
gaping holes in fields green dress.
Like a wasteland great eye sore,
ulcer patch on earthen floor.

Wild flowers no longer grow,
yellow buttercups no heads to show.
Encroaching weeds slow and sure,
field no longer green and pure.

A barren space ugly place,
reflecting only its ruined face.
The field of green once so fair,
wounded, damaged, beyond repair.

Leon Draper

SUBSIDENCE

The water table's got broken legs,
It'll take a lot more than French Polishing,
To smooth over the cracks in its surface,
And to raise it back to supping level.

Clay parched hard as concrete,
New hard-standings, lean-to's and patios built every week,
Blocking surface slopes, natural soaks, and under-soil aquifers,
Recoursing any and all the rain straight away down the drains,
And so, dry as a bone, the brittle ground starts cracking,
Is it any real wonder that foundations are sagging?

Desiccated by scorching summer drought and heat,
Hose-pipe bans could soon be in force,
With dry baths and taps, and standpipes in the street,
Where has all the vital rainwater gone,
That once bathed and turgidified the family seat?
It wasn't spirited away by gargoyles or garden elves,
It was taken into captivity by others, *humans,* just like ourselves,
you'll find it locked up, stocked up, and bottled up by the megamillion,
Abroad and up and down the country,
On hundreds of thousands of supermarket's shelves,
And, what's more,
They will expect *you* to pay *them* for it!

Mel Haebogg

THE OZONE

We are burning holes
in the big blue sky.
The ozone layer
is soon to die.
Chemicals and fumes
fill the air.
Do we the humans
really care.
The sun shines through
not filtered out.
Burns our skin
do we still doubt.
Ultra rays will burn the earth
what of our offspring
what of new birth.
Freakish weather
tidal waves
flooded homes
fresh dug graves.
Dig up the scenery
build new roads
fill it with vehicles
twenty fold.
Worry now,
why who said?
When that time comes
we'll all be dead.

Jacquie Williams

EERIE BEAUTY

Imagine a land green and lush
A plain reaching to the mountains
Horses grazing
Astonishingly quiet
Yet disconcerted we view
The plain's pitted
Concealed wounds gaping beneath
Unhealed by the lapse of time
High explosives violated nature's purity
Generations inheriting soil
Explode-on-impact bomblets cushioned
Waiting
Undetected until another body bloodies the land
And so the ravages of war
Injure and maim
Infested with mines the land lies sterile
A graveyard to these live devices
Wandering livestock unaware of the dangers
Tread firmly, chewing their feed
Until . . .

Clair Chittenden

MOTHER EARTH

Mother Earth what have we done?
Endless wars that nobody's won
The pollution of valleys, rivers and streams
Is this the aim of man's dreams?
The killing of animals for profit and fun
They take pleasure from a loaded gun
Oil slicks that are smothering the sea
Will the whale ever be free?
The planet's in need of repair
But does anyone really care?

Nuclear weapons are out of control
Tearing apart its heart and soul
I want to breathe air that is clean
Live in a world that is oh so green
Forests disappearing out of sight
Do we know what's wrong or what's right?
Stop the rot before it's too late
Can this be our only fate?
Mother Earth what have we done?
What will we leave for our daughter and son?

Nicholas Fletcher

A REGULATED DEATH

A massive death occurred today.
Six tonnes of pears
were buried in the earth
because of EC regulations.
Sell to supermarkets?
Not allowed, and
forbidden to be given away -
a strange and strangulated death.
     Ripe juicy pears
     of pleasing shape
     shovelled down
     to keep top prices up.
A British farmer who had
pruned and tended fruit,
his trade, now had to dig
his produce under -
a quite unnatural
Agricultural Act,
Affront to hunger and to health.
It was a tasteless death,
this burying of food alive.

Marian Reid

167

WHEN WILL WE LEARN

Going going gone like smoke in the air,
causing pollution everywhere. The wind
will carry the problems far, like
nuclear weapons and fumes from cars.
We're killing the planet and people
too, Lord our saviour what can we do?
The time is now or soon the
end, learn to live and love again.
The world is ours to share
together, we must act now or we're
lost forever. So banish all weapons
and CFCs, and inhale the *air* with
the greatest of ease.
Forget about the wars that we've fought,
peace is what our children need taught.
Start from the bottom to rise to the
top, and not one bomb will ever need
drop.

Paul Cushen

POOR WHELK

Plucked from the sea bed in your prime
net and fish market reeking brine
Your one foot reaching out to test the air
of motorway and wagon you had your share
then into Morrisons still alive and whole
on frosted counter you share a day with sole
and plaice and squid and Greenland halibut . . .
. . . your end was near as cockles
all snapped shut.
Then cosmopolitan guy, oh groovy fella
bought you to drop in his paella.

D Clarke

168

FALLOW

They destroy the tree . . .
rip up the root!
Butcher all animals . . .
with joy they shoot!
They trap and snare . . .
deer, badger and hare!
and yet, they can sleep at night!

Who gives them the right to mess with the land.
Squeezing all the blood out of nature in their hand.
They are not God . . . punish them please!
Make mankind fall mercilessly onto his knees!

Adele E McCafferty

THE DESPOILERS

'Only a dune' you will declare,
'All right, I'll strew my debris there!'
An old Z-bed with springs all bent,
My ancient jeans with one leg rent,
A headless doll,
An old toy train
'Oh now it's coming on to rain'
The sea buckthorn is crushed and dying
And heedless of the gulls' shrill crying
The spoilers wreck our lovely land
But who will stop the heedless band.

Shelagh Kinnear Pye

THE ERROR OF YOUR WAYS

How can I believe this is a way of life
Con artists who strike as a way of life
The pick pockets, they steal, without a worry at all
They cause strife amongst even the small

Take me the other day, sitting, having a coffee, without a worry
at all
I looked down, my handbag gone, everything and all
How can I believe, all was gone
I went into shock, I became so small

Why, I thought, why take it all
Even my glasses, complex, no good for all
I have glaucoma, I need those so much
Perhaps they would consider, let their hearts open and touch

Give a little thought, you thieves of this world
Think on, I dare you, it will open up your heart
I will then be able to see once again
Out in the bright sunlight, I'd be grateful then

One day in the future, God will sing you a song
Because your heart would have listened to this song
You will see the error of your ways
And then will live with hope for the rest of your days

Mary Jo West

LET'S KEEP IT GREEN

We have to stop
Before it's too late
With no green to show
We are sealing our fate.

This planet is home
For people to see.
Animals and birds
And large living trees.

We have to look after
This wonderful place.
Before it ends up
Like a planet in space.

We're chopping and cutting
And scarring the land.
If we're not careful
We will only have sand.

When greenery is almost gone
And nothing more to see.
The children of the future
Will ask . . . teacher, what's a tree?

And when you read my poem
Think of my little rhyme.
Plant some seeds, for future years
I'm sure, you have the time . . .

T B Rees

BOSNIA

Fragile peace in Bosnia amid
Snow-mantled mountains and
Mine-tapped valleys that once
Rang with rustic voices . . . now
Lie in winter silence's icy grip
Of fear-filled days and nights,
When muffled cries of owls, indistinguishable
From human pain, secretly search
A landscape of misery, in vain . . .
For furry prey long gone to earth
To seek their solace in burrows deep
Among decomposing mortal remains
Of someone's sons and daughters . . .
No more the joy of procreation when
Above ground nation slaughters nation . . .
And there is no reconciliation . . .
Men's hearts are dead amongst the dying . . .
So what's the use of trying . . .
Best to sleep . . .
Cocooned in warm brown earth beneath
The conflict and the pain's blind ignorance . . .
And dream of sunlit season's joyous return . . .
Reborn in nature's eternal summer promise . . .
She will provide the balm and healing comfort.

Jean Makin

TRY A TASTE OF INDIA

Try a taste of India.
Sip a bit of Spain.
Chew a while on Tanzania.
Tip Chile down the drain.

Munch on Madagascar.
Eat up Ecuador.
Swallow down all Cape Town.
Gulp Asia and then more.

Open the door of the Philippines.
Take out a cold Tasmania.
Grab Israel from the fruit bowl.
Bin shrivelled, old Romania.

Then, casually dressed in China,
Switch on South Korea.
Place Columbia on Burma.
Let Taiwan assail your ear.

The programme on the telly
Will show floods, disease and drought.
'Damn foreigners!' You'll say out loud,
'Here! Leave those stories out!'

The world within will hear you
Will groan and grumble and mew
Till with upward surge
It'll finally purge
You
In its last adieu.

Bruce Alexander

CONSERVATION

We're all responsible in some way for environmental pollution.
There are many things we see mentioned that could help in a
      solution.
Perhaps one that causes most offence is in the form of traction,
And yet to recommend alternatives may not have a
      favourable reaction.
For there's investment in transport that uses fuels that offend.
Electrically propelled or gas energised many would recommend.
It's ironic that the oil that's transported from places that retain
      the wealth
Should end up with disastrous results on other shores, a direct
      threat to health.
And so fishermen who depend on catches from the sea in
      order to survive
See much of what they depend on contaminated, or just not
      alive.
Birds become oil bound, and some consume the oil.
Conservationists help, but many birds do not survive, despite
      the never ending toil.
They have become victims of what could be termed a human greed.
For the oil in question will eventually be processed to provide
      a growing need.
To ask someone to give up their car has been suggested in some
      measure
But many are so attached it's an obsession, the one thing that
      they treasure.
It seems that until vehicles that allow clean air are in production
There'll be the need for more safety measures that are recommended for
      oil tanker construction.
We should be considering future generations instead of just the present day
Using all options so that we could say pollution has long since gone away.
The dream is that powers that be and politicians will give a
      thought in this respect,
But no doubt it will remain a dream, is it too much to expect?

Reg Morris

MAN'S MITIGATION

Early in the life of this our planet earth
Each and every species was programmed at birth
For their survival and care of habitat too
Such a natural and sensible thing to do

Both in competition and co-operation
All parties worked to maintain that situation
Individual gain never was an issue
So different from what we usually do

One sad day a surprising occurrence took place
Homo Sapien descendants were in disgrace
The first couple of the human family tree
Each from their programmed ways decided to break free

The serpent and fruit each played their part in this shame
Though the couple for ever really got the blame
As the way now is for individual gain
Forget the habitat get all your can obtain

Man has been told just what to do love his neighbour
Think of others and their world beyond his front door
On us all survival really depends it's true
Though unfortunate as it is we now can't do

But a hopeful future is a reality
Science can change your ways and personality
Well of course it all sounds simply too fantastic
Yes until you delve into the microscopic.

Harry Derx

175

WHY?

World disasters bring a tear to my eye,
God, are you listening?
A simple question asked,
as the tear on my cheek is glistening.

I hold my breath to imagine death,
there is no part inside,
that you can start to feel the pain they hold,
when there's nowhere left to hide.
Tiny babies whimper still,
when the mother's life has ended,
Mother Nature's been condemned.
When she should have been commended.
I have no thoughts of how we came,
to live our lives like this,
the human race has made life hell,
when it should have been pure bliss.

Michelle Chrystie

DECAY OF THE WORLD

'Look at the state of the world today'
Is what a lot of people say,
But none of them will stop,
Causing the decay,
With the chemicals we use every day,
And the rubbish, that we throw away,
It's destroying our beautiful world,
What will we do,
When it's died away,
We will have nowhere,
Left to play.

Amanda Jervis

THE BENEVOLENCE OF NATURE

Fog - of mind, of attitude
Where oh where has progress led us?
But to plunder and consume as food
The benevolence of nature

Intelligence - apparent or real?
Invention, growth, science
Why oh why do we steal?
From the benevolence of nature

Impact - oh yes, oh yes my friend
Indulge away and be deaf to a cry
Let no-one ever pretend
We deserve the benevolence of nature

Sorrow - reflect and forgive?
Foolish, impatient man are we
In irreverence we dain to live
Within the benevolence of nature

Martin Hazell

MASKED FUTURE

Behold her! This rounded earth, giver always,
Never the taker.
Yet, she is sucked dry.
Hers is the final holocaust.
It is this rounded earth, this smiling planet,
That is at the rainbow's end.
Mankind's pot of gold.
Our smiling planet needs an ark,
It needs a Noah, and a dove to
Send out to find an olive leaf.

Gerry Kenny

PIPE DREAM: CRUDE OIL

To gain its riches some men kill:
Sp*oil* fauna and flora with overspill.
If speed's a drug; this substance brings thrills.
Reap the handicap harvest bored by the drill:
We're all content to take our fill.
But w*hose* generation picks up the bill?

Sally Walding

SAVE OUR LAND

They're pulling down a lot of trees,
to build another road.
The old ones not enough they say,
to take the load.

Tell that to all the squirrels,
badgers and animals that roam.
Whose ancestors for centuries,
have made the wood their home.

The flowers and the shrubs that grew,
in the wood as if by instinct.
Are now to be decimated,
and may eventually become extinct.

It's man's permanent desire,
to prosper and opt for greed.
Giving no thought of the consequence,
or considering others' need.

So let's preserve our countryside,
and all our wiles employ.
To thwart the men and women,
who would plant and field destroy.

B Eyre

NOWHERE TO GO

Who stands beside to take their hands
when they cry out in need?
Who tends to mothers in despair
with tiny mouths to feed?

Who in this world knows they are born?
Who holds out loving arms?
Where is the gentle smiling face
or where the voice that calms?

No warmth and comfort of a home.
No pillows for each head.
Just tragic lives of hopelessness
and holes to leave the dead!

No strength to stand. Nowhere to go.
No food or drink today.
They lay down in their weariness,
too tired to even pray.

So loudly every voice speaks out
and calls 'Oh help us please!'
So many just don't hear at all,
safe in their life of ease.

When day and night are all the same
and pain knows no relief.
I turn away and do not share
or understand their grief.

Oh heart and conscience are you there?
Bring trouble to this brow.
May shame awake this sleeping soul
and use this body now!

John Christopher Cole

TOO LATE?

Who dug that hole
in the ozone
who sprayed that aerosol
What have you done!
Car exhausts and chimneys pollute the air
rubbish discarded with little care
dirty sea
deserted beach
everyone covered so the sun can't reach
And burn a hole through our skin
through a gap, where the ozone should have
been
So now we re-cycle tin, plastic and glass
we've finally learnt, at long last!
But can we wash the sea
or clean the air
or mend the damage we caused there.

Kathryn L Cowling

DISAPPEARING WORLD

We have our land and free fresh air
And yet we still don't seem to care
About pollution in the sky
Or rivers that will soon run dry
Of fogs and fumes in city streets
Of poison waste we bury deep

Now where have all the forests gone?
They've been cut down to build upon
They say we need more homes and shops
With car parks and new office blocks
We need the highways and the roads
To take the ever increasing loads.

But ask yourself a question thus
What happens to the rest of us?
I do not ask this all alone
I ask for those who have lost their homes
For creatures on the land and sea
Why can't we live in harmony?

Gillian Conners

PLANET EARTH

Planet Earth from bygone ages
Developed slowly, in controlled stages
This evolution - of God's creation
Produced, the concept - of every nation
Every thought, and every dream
Were part and parcel - of that scene
First and foremost, came mankind
God's vision - of a master mind
Intelligence! Beyond the norm
Disciples - of our Lord were born
A concept! Full of good intention
Rewards - for all! Too great to mention
Providing, for our every need
Not! Programmed - was the evil, greed
A malfunction of the human mind
The greatest setback - for mankind
Manifest! In seats of power
Human greed, thrives by the hour
A retrogression, to days of old
World leaders - worship Gods of Gold.

Ernie Martin

EARTH

Soft ebony,
And diamond stars,
Surround, our sapphire earth,
With golden sun,
And silver moon,
A treasure, of great worth.

She's beautiful,
In every way,
Revolving, here in space.
From sparkling sea,
To country lane,
Her perfect, living grace.

So carelessly,
We've poisoned her,
Man alone's to blame.
We buried her,
In concrete tomb,
She must, be free again.

Then fragrantly,
She'll bloom anew,
Her guardian, we should be.
Keep faith with her;
Our fragile earth;
Our jewel, in ebony.

Diana Mary Gale

LEGAL VANDALS

The fields once peacefully were seen
Covering the land with green;
Farmhands worked to raise the crops
Needed to supply our shops.

Wild flowers grew in great profusion;
Animals lived without confusion;
Rabbits, hares and harvest mice
Prospered in this paradise.

Time came when the greed of man
Caused the forming of a plan
To strip the fields and lay them bare;
Instead - build houses everywhere.

But first some traces of the past
Were excavated to the last
And bones of ancient man were found
Buried underneath the ground.

Then one day in bleak November
Came a day we'll all remember;
To the fields, in place of tractors,
Came machines of the contractors.

Stakes and ropes marked out the land;
JCBs moved in as planned;
The legal vandals of our day
Had come to take our peace away.

Geoff Tullett

BARRIERS UNVEILED

The glorious days through summer haze
Beam bounties manifold
So we acclaim with shouts of praise
At wonders to behold.

In His great wisdom He decreed
That life sun's substance needs
To fuel and clothe and breathe and feed
So cultivate new seeds.

And when from heat we cry, 'Enough!'
The good Lord sends us rain
To quench our thirsty water troughs
And cool the scalding plains.

These gifts sent freely from on high
We take as promise due
But in return acidify
With fumes and gases new.

So now these rays burst through a screen
Removed by man's misdeeds
And chilling mist destroys our dreams
With putrefying streams.

Lesley Coates

RIVERWORLD

Visualise a lonely hillside
split by a steep gully
and realise that here
is a womb of the world
where the mother earth
gives birth to a thrusting babe
who bursting with liquid life
bubbles its infant cries
in a rock strewn cot.

Enlarging in time and space
the baby grows into adult life
full of aquatic power
flowing to the waiting sea.

Dark woods drop to the river bank
as water flows past meadows reflected in their mirror
and a paddling heron
takes a calculated step
towards an unsuspecting fish.

Now at the dark frontier
river life falters
as man's poisons pollute the waters
spewing from factories
which sweat their foul waste
into the defenceless watercourse
where the materialistic world
of profit at any price
ignores the dead and dying fish
who are the sad sacrifice
upon the tarnished altar
of big fat dividends and cost effective gains.

Stephen Gyles

STOP THE ROT

Planet earth is slowly dying
Suffering quietly
Unless this course is halted
We shall sorry be

Politicians seem remote
Nothing much is done
When it's too late they will know
Talking hasn't won

If it doesn't make a profit
Then it isn't any good
Just how wrong these men are
Is clearly understood

Children now will bear the brunt
Of all our past mistakes
For their sakes if no other
Put a stop, apply the brakes

Man is his own worst enemy
With power, lust and greed
Do something now and stop the rot
There is an urgent need.

Verity Denton

CRIMES AGAINST THE PLANET

There are glaciers on this planet
That are retreating very fast
They are telling all mankind
Our way of living cannot last

Dr Beeching with his axe
Cutting freight and passenger tracks
Ten thousand trees sacrificed for a by-pass
Seventy thousand tons of oil spilled in the sea
If this kind of thing goes on
A grim future for this planet I foresee.

If man persists in his polluting
Of this precious thing called air
In time there will be no safe haven
For living creatures anywhere.

W G Palmer

NO!

The sun is blood upon the hill.
The grass is brown, the earth is still.
No breath of air, no cloud in sight
No jumping frog, no bird in flight.
The ground is sand beneath my feet
While all around me are asleep.
No water now, no brimming cup,
What will it take to wake them up.
No more the crests of waves to ride.
No dams required to stem the tide
They are but bastions on a barren countryside.
The sun is blood upon the hill,
The land is dead, the earth is still.

Constance I Roper

TAKING LIBERTY WITH GREEN

We are not brave
Just flesh puppets
Pink brutal insects
Upright locusts
Tearing, in biblical mimicry
The flesh (burnt money crisp)
As she orbits
In time
Cutting her ark
Across the sky

There are some
Who carry the lamps of life
Beneath folds of defiance
To the failing mad machinery
And the stained brittle breezes
Or hollow oily seas that crash on empty shores
In new born darkness
Fresh and new (like clean dollar bills)
Child of light's laziness
Settling on the trees
As if a roof
The lessening days here are edged in steel
As the forests fall, quiet . . .
And there will be nothing,
To mark our passing . . .

Defies description
What we have done.

Nik Harding

HAY - THE BEST

Don't delay - when all around
Nature is calling you - come
See the stately trees and glades
All grown for you chum.
They are humming a stately song
As the breeze caresses the leaves
The grass today will make nice hay
If the farmer don't spoil the surface.
It's not mother earth he's wooing
With his raping of the land
What gold enough this grass is
If left to grow with its own will.
Nature will always know better
Than any man can till.
Sweetest smell of all is
The sweetness of the hay
Made even sweeter, on a June day.
As it's cut, turned and kissed
by the friendly sun.
The gentle breeze from heaven
Is all it needs - till done.
I do so wish the people who
Have this earth to tend - could
See the beauty round them
Not spoiling the tilth and the seed.
Leaving the earth with its wonder
To send forth its own life
Freely given to us for support
For our good - instead of our strife.

Pamela J Scott

SINS AGAINST NATURE

Sheep's brains fed to vegetarian cattle
has nature in an uproar, prepared to battle.
The primate man thinks he knows it all
with arrogance he heads for a fatal fall.
BSE emerges in the human throng.
The bovine species did no wrong.
Man hunts the dolphins, kills the whales.
In respect and understanding he sadly fails.
If subsistence, the name of the game,
Nature would understand and not blame.
Men call it wholesome, social sport
in red coats chasing frightened foxes fraught.
Selfish spouses adorned in mink.
The lives of rare species nearly at the brink.
Elephants hunted for tusks, tigers for skins.
Trawled, netted and hooked those with fins.
This is another kind of Sodom and Gomorra
Soon there will be no nature and no tomorrow.

Nina Knights

CND .. ?

'Can we go to the park today, Mummy?
You promised that we could
Can we go to the park today
And run through the grass and the wood
So cool, so pleasant and green.
But Mummy, I forget they dropped the bomb
And this shelter is my home, I do think
Those rotten Russians are so mean . . .'

Jackie Callow

190

THE EARTH'S PRAYER

Compassionate summer garden,
Lend your naked frame to the cruel hours.

You once healed tribes without judgement
But now your natural beauty drowns
In a torrent of cement and greasy machinery:
An onslaught of intense energy
Penetrating deep inside the earth's hollow shell.

Your green lungs filter dark polluted skies
And your unheard cries
Remain cold echoes in time's hostile embrace.

A ragged necklace of hedges and trees once twisted
And turned for miles around,
Yet now they are wrapped with wire
Which tears and cuts deep into your throat.
You patiently observe the stains of progress
Staring with horror at the gaping hole
We have punched through the sky

You struggle for breath
And endure each slow century

In another scene, the great red eye sinks lower
Embarrassed at the surrounding chaos:
Cities become hazy with thick dust
As infectious crowds breath hard on your aching sides.

The golden dream of yesterdays stay with us
Giving us hope amongst the sordid findings of a new age.

Peter Harris

191

OUR BEAUTIFUL WORLD

People who kill for gain, have no shame
Whenever there is a profit to be made
Indirectly, we are all to blame
For not protesting against the sale

We sit in our home and watch TV
Tut in disgust, when they fell another tree
We don't want windows made of UPVC
So where does the wood come from, you tell me.

Many wild animals are on the decline
It is up to us, to make sure they survive.
Once they are dead and no longer exist
You can be sure, we'll be next on the list.

A lot of our cities resemble the jungle
The strongest rise and the weakest tumble
Leaving the scavengers to pick at their bones
Where they rot and decay in the undergrowth

To escape the smell of the rotting flesh
Those who can afford to, move where the air is fresh
What will they do, when there is no more room
Buy themselves a ticket, to fly to the moon

Leaving behind them the rest of mankind
To live in the world that they have designed
If man can do this, to his fellow man
What chance have animals, in another land

Unless we radically change our ways
Of living our lives each and every single day
We are going to end up like the dinosaurs
No, not extinct, but on all fours.

Linda Tosney

POLLUTION OF EARTH

We are all polluting,
Our lovely planet Earth,
Air is being poisoned,
Exhaust fumes blowing dirt,
Aeroplanes and aerosols,
Pour out poisoned fumes,
Creating breathing problems,
We put ourselves in tombs,
Water too, we poison,
With chemicals and oil,
Spillage from great tankers,
We must become more loyal,
To this lovely world we have,
Given to us free,
This is God's own garden,
Given to you and me,
Spraying crops and poisoning,
The vegetation there,
Then we all consume the food,
We must be more aware,
Of what we all are doing,
To the earth, the air, the sea,
Stop these awful actions,
It starts with you and me,
Think of the consequences,
And look ahead of time,
For what we do to mother earth,
Is such a dreadful crime.

Janette Campbell

A LETTER TO MOTHER EARTH

Dearest, dearest, serene, mother earth,
you wonderful, vibrant planet who gave us all birth,
in this brief, apologetic letter, I'm trying to say,
that I'm sorry we humans abuse you each day!

Can you forgive us the innumerable wars,
of which greed, hatred and hunger have been the cause?
Can you forgive us the mindless destruction too,
inflicted 'pon the beauty given to us by you?

I'm sorry for us harming each of your rainforests,
arrayed with splendour, like an enormous florists,
and the wonderful creatures unnecessarily destroyed,
oh, yes, dear earth, you have every right to be annoyed!

For the ores and minerals that we've torn from your heart,
of which the list's too numerous for me to even start,
For the testing and experimenting with chemicals and bombs,
and the irrevocable creation of a worldly maelstrom!

We're not fit, dear earth, to dwell 'pon your face,
methinks we should inhabit a much hotter place,
yes, to hell with us all, for we've surely let you known,
we've damned ourselves, and in our own evil we'll drown!

So, dearest mother earth, I'll close my pathetic letter,
knowing that our self-centred ways won't get any better,
One day, when it's too late, you'll abandon us anon,
and then we'll have time to ask, 'What *on earth* have we done?'

PS Don't give up on us just yet, because we need you still,
we'll *try* to improve our behaviour, we promise we will,
without you dear earth mother, we cannot survive,
without your resilience and wisdom, we wouldn't be alive!

With fond regards and respect from one of your inhabitants.

David Brasier

A MERE TOURIST

The air I breathe may stink a touch,
the sea be less than blue.
It doesn't really matter much
I'm only passing through.
And though I'd like a longer stay,
one life is all I've got.
So live it up from day to day
and let the planet rot.
Let mother earth become a vile
and bloody, filthy mess.
I'm leaving in a little while,
and couldn't care less.

M P Brown

THE CARETAKER

The flag of peace, truth and love,
Flutters in the breeze,
So take the oath of freedom,
To protect, the earth, and seas,
Nature, appoints us all,
Caretakers of this earth,
To respect, the animals, plants, and trees,
Even the air we breathe,
The earth gives food, for all the nations,
A legacy, for future generations,
So pull down the boundaries of hate,
Do it now, do not wait,
Protect, the things we really need,
And do away with hate, and greed . . .

J Smith

THE KEY TO UNDERSTANDING

Softly blows the wind of change,
As it crosses the boundary between love and hate,
Delving deeply into our souls, like a surgical implement,
Until we, gnawed and raw from intrusion,
Resign ourselves completely to its mighty force.

As we succumb to its overpowering strength,
We greedily prepare to indulge in the fruits of its labour;
The knowledge that has so far eluded us,
Hoping that we can learn from it,
And make the changes necessary in ourselves.

For the chosen and earmarked of us,
Stand to receive its special treatment,
And like Pandora's box it will open,
Revealing the pleasures and evils,
Of the reality that we call life.

And then we might be able to say yes,
This is it, this is the feeling I've striven for,
At long last I've attained the knowledge I've been looking for,
And can now look down on the poor misguided fools,
Who are still searching.

And with this knowledge comes the slow comprehension,
That it is us who keep the homeless where they are,
For they, unlike our enlightened selves, are in need of deliverance,
Deliverance not from the vileness of street life,
But from us, the ones in power.
And so it is not the homeless we should pity,
It is ourselves, for not understanding.

Tracy Clark

SAVAGERY

Violence walks upon our streets
and parades itself upon our screens,
for we don't teach our children
what truth and kindness means.

They do not learn compassion,
they aren't told what is fair.
We leave them in the darkness
with no ray of sunshine there.

Now their bodies are polluted
by the poisons in our air,
it floats around our cities,
but no-one seems to care.

Put all these things together
and they make a ghastly pot,
which wipes out all the kindness
and the good things we've forgot.

Now we let our little children
learn to swear and fight and steal,
with no thought of the harm to others,
nor how our old folks feel.

So we must put them back on course,
get the whole world back to rights,
give up the greed that's in our hearts,
and stop those needless fights.

Daf Richards

POOH

When children play
On holiday
A safe, clean site is the key,
We usually reach
A smelly beach
Where sewage pours into the sea.

Beaches are dumps
For squishy, brown lumps
Where waters froth and foam,
This with bad taste
Of other yuk waste
Makes us want to rush home.

We wonder why
The animals die
People ignore the connection,
Just from one swim
The outcome is grim -
Illness, disease and infection.

So, what do you do
When faced with pooh
Floating by your side?
Stay composed
Keep your mouth closed
And *never* open it wide.

Celia Hooker

EARTH'S MOURN

The land cries out to breathe,
Crushed by concrete,
One more brick,
One more house,
Just another needed street.

Green leaves aching to be free,
Pushed down hard.
One more brick,
One more house,
Open countryside now barred.

Homeless creatures die alone,
No more space.
One more brick,
One more house,
Completing the property race.

No animals, no trees, no plants,
Not even a blade of grass.
Everywhere bricks,
Everywhere houses,
How long will our future last?

Lee Brewin

NOAH'S DREAM

In the space between moonshine and dawn,
Noah's unexplained
Dream was born:
Of shining turtles with watery eyes,
and hump-backed whales gliding by,
Of fire coated tigers
With snake-like tails,
and proud strutting peacocks
With feathers like sails,
and many others,
Swept aside
By glassy towers
Built up by unknown powers.
He watched them all fade,
Like sleeping flowers,
Beaten down
By acidic showers.

Melanie Batley

REMAINS OF THE FOREST

Striding through the trees
I can feel the coldest breeze
I search through the poisonous rain
Trying not to feel the pain
Once this forest was pure
Now there is no cure
There is no place to hide
For the forest has simply died
Where did man go wrong?
Was it because we were too strong
And where I stand alone
Is the place I called home.

Ben Crossland

INFORMATION

We hope you have enjoyed reading this book - and that you will continue to enjoy it in the coming years.

If you like reading and writing poetry drop us a line, or give us a call, and we'll send you a free information pack.

Write to

Arrival Press Information
1-2 Wainman Road
Woodston
Peterborough
PE2 7BU